Dear Reader:

The book you are about to read is the latest bestseller from the St. Martin's True Crime Library, the imprint the *New York Times* calls "the leader in true crime!" Each month, we offer you a fascinating account of the latest, most sensational crime that has captured the national attention. St Martin's is the publisher of bestselling true crime author and crime journalist Kieran Crowley, who explores the dark, deadly links between a prominent Manhattan surgeon and the disappearance of his wife fifteen years earlier in THE SURGEON'S WIFE. Carlton Smith's COLD-BLOODED details the death of a respected attorney—and the secret, sordid life of his wife. In Edgar Award-nominated DARK DREAMS, legendary FBI profiler Roy Hazelwood and bestselling crime author Stephen G. Michaud shine light on the inner workings of America's most violent and depraved murderers. In the book you now hold, A WIFE'S REVENGE, Eric Francis tells the story of Susan Wright, who stabbed her husband to end his alleged domestic abuse.

St. Martin's True Crime Library gives you the stories behind the headlines. Our authors take you right to the scene of the crime and into the minds of the most notorious murderers to show you what really makes them tick. St. Martin's True Crime Library paperbacks are better than the most terrifying thriller, because it's all true! The next time you want a crackling good read, make sure it's got the St. Martin's True Crime Library logo on the spine—you'll be up all night!

Charles E. Spicer, Jr.
Executive Editor, St. Martin's True Crime Library

St. Martin's
True Crime Library Titles by
Eric Francis

The Dartmouth Murders

Broken Vows

A WIFE'S REVENGE

ERIC FRANCIS

St. Martin's Paperbacks

A WIFE'S REVENGE

Copyright © 2005 by Eric Francis.

Cover photo of bed © Kim Steele/Getty Images.
Photo of woman © Pat Sullivan/AP Wide World Photos.

ISBN: 0-312-98519-3
EAN: 80312-98519-6

Printed in the United States of America

St. Martin's Paperbacks edition / June 2005

St. Martin's Paperbacks are published by St. Martin's Press, 175 Fifth Avenue, New York, NY 10010.

10 9 8 7 6 5 4 3 2

AUTHOR'S NOTE

Because of the way the case unfolded, the prosecution directed at Susan Wright did not need to spell out the entire sequence of events nor all the exact details as to how they thought she had murdered her husband.

As a result, the first three chapters contain descriptions of the circumstances surrounding the death and burial of Jeffrey Wright that are products of the author's imagination based upon the prosecution's theories of murder and motive as they were presented both inside the courtroom and in press interviews outside of it.

The only person capable of knowing with absolute certainty what happened is the defendant, Susan Wright, and, as the reader will learn, she has consistently given an account of her husband's killing and the events which precipitated and followed it that is completely at odds with the version advanced by the prosecution. Nonetheless, a jury of her peers found the prosecution's case compelling beyond a reasonable doubt and unanimously convicted her.

The descriptions of specific actions, thoughts, feelings, and motivations that are ascribed to Susan Wright in the opening chapters are written as the author imagined they would be if she had indeed acted in a manner consistent with the prosecution's theories of a premeditated murder. The scenario that is described is one possibility as to how such a killing might have occurred and it should not be taken as either undisputed fact nor as the author's personal conclusion as to what actually transpired.

At the time of this writing Susan Wright's request for a new trial was still pending before the Texas Court of Appeals.

The material in this book derives from public records, personal interviews, and news reports from the *Houston Chronicle,* KHOU, KTRK, KPRC, CNN, Fox News, CBS News *48 Hours,* Oxygen Network's *Snapped,* the Associated Press, *ABC News Good Morning America,* Court TV, *The National Law Journal, Houston Business Journal, Texas Lawyer, Fort Worth Star-Telegram, Austin American-Statesman,* and *People* magazine among others.

A WIFE'S REVENGE

A MURDER IS ANNOUNCED

Several hours had passed since attorney Neal Davis had been hurriedly called out for an unusual weekend meeting with a desperate client—a pretty, frightened, suburban mother of two young children on Houston's tranquil northwestern edge.

But now, as Saturday afternoon turned to evening, the horror of what he had seen sticking partially out of the ground beside her patio, where the family dog had been digging, was still causing him to shiver as he walked through the front doors of the Harris County District Attorney's Office.

The Intake Division staff who'd pulled weekend duty knew immediately that something was wrong just by looking at Davis. His hands were shaking uncontrollably as he turned over a business card from his prestigious Houston law firm and struggled to write the woman's Berry Tree Drive address on the back of it.

Davis stammered that he was a lawyer, but because of attorney–client privilege he couldn't tell the authorities who he was representing. Handing his card to Assistant District Attorney Terese Buess, Davis paused and then, in a spooked voice, he got to the point of his visit. "There's a dead body at this address and I can't say anything else."

PROLOGUE

At the end of that bloody evening there was only one person remaining—one spouse, one killer, one survivor, one witness. She would be the only one who knew with certainty what had really taken place. But even to her, looking back, the whole thing seemed like it had been an out-of-body experience—a foggy troubled dream.

When she was finally forced to explain why it had all unfolded in such a confused and tangled manner, her reasons would be nearly as unnerving as what she had actually done. She would detail a life completely at odds with what her family and her friends thought they had known of her, a life of private despair hidden in plain view behind a façade of pleasant tranquillity, a beautifully wrapped package containing dark secrets that had brought her to the breaking point.

But the search for an explanation would also fall to the authorities—police, detectives, medical examiners, and prosecutors—and when they sifted through what remained and put the blood-soaked pieces of the puzzle back together, they came to a very different conclusion about what had really happened to an unsuspecting husband one winter evening in Houston . . .

1

There were a lot of things on Jeffrey Wright's mind that Texas afternoon, but dying wasn't one of them.

It was the first week of January, with memories of New Year's Eve still fresh, and temperatures along the Gulf of Mexico had soared clear into the 70s. But over the weekend, winter bit back hard. Houston had plunged nearly to the freezing point, barely eking out a high of 40 degrees on Sunday.

Now, on Monday, January 13, 2003, that unusual burst of Arctic air had passed, and as Jeffrey Wright drove his large blue pickup truck home, Houston was beginning to heat back up.

Jeff was beginning to heat back up too. Returning to work on Mondays was always a drag, but as a successful salesman, Jeff knew enough to take things as they came. He'd dealt with retailers and wholesalers, moving carpet and tile orders all day long. But on Monday afternoons following work, he had a method for releasing the stress of the week's first workday. Before he returned home to his pretty young wife, his little boy, and his baby daughter, he took out all the day's tensions at boxing lessons.

That was the idea, anyway. The problem with the boxing-lessons theory of relaxation was that the lessons weren't all Jeff was taking. He'd also managed to score several lines' worth of cocaine on his way to the boxing ring. Jeff was a big guy, 6' 3" and 220 pounds. He could hold up his end in the ring, but he was also 34 years old now and an amateur. There were several younger, fitter guys at the gym who could slam like a mule, so Jeff liked the sharp edge that the coke gave him when it was his turn to slug it out. In fact, there was a lot about that little edge that he'd discovered he liked . . . and now it was becoming clear that lately he'd been liking it a bit too much.

The coke Jeff had been snorting his way through wasn't free. But each time he had a chance to score some, he'd reached into his wallet and handed over a wad of cash. Jeff had been doing well enough financially, but he certainly wasn't the richest guy on the block and this was an expensive habit that he really couldn't afford.

On paper Jeff's life looked solidly middle-class. He had a wife, two kids, two cars, and a clean little house on a quiet side street in one of the newer neighborhoods on Houston's northwestern fringe. But there were a lot of bills, a lot of the usual suburban pressures—and in the seemingly pedestrian world of marketing carpet and tile, there were plenty of other up-and-coming young salespeople who wouldn't mind carving a slice out of Jeff's clientele to further their own middle-class American dreams.

Jeff could be a hard worker, when he wanted to be, but he could also slip on his party animal hat. That tendency, along with the cocaine, was taking him on some pricey binges that were now coming home to roost.

The drugs were a vestige of Jeff's years as a young single guy working his way up in the business, first in Austin and then Houston. Over the years, in a series of legendary blowouts, Jeff and his buddies would get together and go for days on end without sleep taking partying into the realm of extreme sport. Anything went. Alcohol. Drugs. Hookers. Two hookers at a time. The point was to create another crazed scene to remember through a haze of hangovers and knowing inside jokes with lifelong pals.

But Jeff had grown up, a bit anyway. He was making increasingly good money for a guy who was just then pushing thirty. In his quieter moments he'd begun to see himself settling down one day and making a real life for himself. Then one day in 1997 he found her by accident.

She was among a group of friends on a sun-drenched ribbon of sand on the Gulf of Mexico. Susan Lucille Wyche was a striking 21-year-old blonde, pretty enough to have posed for the tourist poster of Galveston Beach that afternoon.

Jeff had struck up a gregarious conversation with the husband of one of Susan's best friends. Susan had checked Jeff out but, still a bit on the shy side around older men, hadn't spoken to him. Later, getting back to her car in the parking area, Susan found Jeff's business card tucked under her windshield wiper. She called him and invited him to dinner.

Jeff was quickly smitten with Susan, and she loved the attention. She'd had a sheltered upbringing thirty miles outside of Houston in the rural railroad junction town of Tomball. She'd done all the usual Norman Rockwell small-town America things a good girl should do from Brownies to church youth groups. At Jersey Village High School she'd steered clear of the sports teams and the teen hang-out scene, preferring instead to curl up at home and watch movies with her mom. But as soon as she was old enough to move she'd wanted to get out of the house and get closer to the bright lights of America's fourth largest city just over the horizon.

At first, the bright lights got a little too intense as Susan quickly found the casting call is always open for perky blonde 18-year-olds at Houston's strip clubs. Every Saturday for eight weeks Susan, the recent high-school graduate, strode onto the bar under the strobe lights in nothing but a G-string as eager guys of all ages passed her bills. The dare over, money in hand, Susan decided she didn't like topless dancing and signed up for classes at a community college looking to eventually become a nurse.

A job at a hair salon followed, but school was proving expensive and time-consuming. Eventually Susan quit for awhile and found more lucrative work as a waitress. Then, one day at the beach, Jeff left his card on her windshield.

Susan liked going out with Jeff. He was actually quite sweet when she got him away from his marauding pack of drinking buddies. He'd had a lot of experience, he knew all the restaurants, he was worldly and went to elaborate efforts to take her nice places.

Jeff was also funny and above all with Susan he was charming. He called her every day, wanting to see her as often as possible. Privately he told his friends who he'd been bingeing his way across Houston's bayous with that this time he'd met "the one"—the woman he wanted to marry, the woman he wanted to settle down with and have kids. It was a domestic vision of Jeff that his pals had a hard time taking seriously at first but he was increasingly saying that he wanted to make it happen.

Something did happen in short order that threw the future into even sharper focus—Susan discovered she was pregnant. She'd had doubts about whether Jeff was really too old for her. Jeff had doubts about whether he was really ready to change course and settle down. It took some soul-searching on both their parts but late in the game, with Susan sitting next to him in his pickup truck, obviously eight months pregnant, in the fall of 1998, Jeff had leaned over and handed her a ring. "Will you marry me?" he asked. Susan, tears welling, had said yes. Jeff would later tell his friends that Susan's acceptance of his offer and his decision to step back from the party scene had probably saved his life.

Two weeks later in a small ceremony with a few close family members and friends outside of Houston they had made it official. Any elaborate honeymoon would have to wait, there was so much to get in order ahead of the baby, so that night the pair celebrated their wedding with a dinner at the Outback Steakhouse in Magnolia. It wasn't every girl's dream of the ultimate romantic venue, but the whole idea of being a wife and mother was actually Susan's dream and that night she was firmly on her way to realizing it.

Baby Bradley arrived and the Wrights moved into a small brick three-bedroom house in the White Oak Bend subdivision within the Cypress–Fairbanks section of Houston. "Cy-Fair" was known as a good area to live and to a lesser extent White Oak Bend was considered an okay neighborhood. Built in the 1980s with a half-dozen curving streets carving up a square parcel of land, 200 homes, many, like the Wrights', surrounded by little brick walls, had been stacked in so tightly next to each other that from the air it looked kind of like a tree-filled corporate office that had been cubicled. But it was the kind of subdivision where young couples bought their first homes, and that's what Jeff and Susan were there to do.

Jeff liked being a husband and a father. He even bragged about his wife and his kids at work. He liked the image and the aura of stability that doing all the right kinds of family-guy things gave him. That image didn't hurt him when it came to doing business. But neither did his more selfish side.

If people were prepared to admire Jeff's regular-guy earnestness, then he could put that forward with pride. But if friends or clients liked to party, talk sports, maybe stop in for an hour at one of Houston's many, many topless bars and check out the eye candy, then Jeff could effortlessly switch gears.

In that regard Jeff seemed to reflect some of the inherent schizophrenia of his adopted home town. Houston can be a bastion of moral conservatism, the buckle on the Bible Belt, where residents can talk about their personal relationships with Jesus in public with a straight face seldom seen outside places like Salt Lake City. But at the same time, Houston has more strip clubs and topless bars, and consequently more strippers and strip club patrons, than any other city in the country—at least double the number of similar establishments in Las Vegas.

Like the city itself, Jeff thought he was adequately juggling those two sides of his own life. If the more puritanical were impressed by family values, then Jeff had those in abundance. He could trot out the wife and kids in suburbia as proof. If the audience was more interested in the wild side of things, well then, Jeff could slyly mention that in years past his hot little wife used to be a topless dancer.

These days it was Susan, the former topless dancer turned suburban housewife, who was putting the most pressure on Jeff to rein it all in and get his act together.

Susan came across great in public. She actually made Jeff look good, especially when he got together with his family and friends. But in private Susan could turn on him, and the vices she objected to were all the ones he really enjoyed and would have the hardest time giving up.

He had no intention of changing any of his habits anytime soon. He was an adult. He was his own man. He was a respectable enough guy, and if he liked to smoke a joint once in a while to relax, that was really nobody's business but his. He liked the euphoric high that came with the coke. He enjoyed slipping into the padded leather seats of the strip clubs and watching this year's crop of nubile talents teeter past in skyscraper-high platform heels and very little else.

He could stuff a lot of singles into a well slung G-string and, despite the hypothetical existence of the city of Houston's "three-foot rule," he knew that with a big enough wad of cash and a well-phrased whisper into the ear of the cutie writhing in his lap, there were times he could end up in a much more private setting spending some real quality time with the Miss Texas–wannabe of the moment.

Lately Jeff had spent too much money on the partying, especially on the cocaine, but he figured some of that came with the holiday season. He'd actually gotten overextended by several thousand dollars—but that could happen to anybody, and it irritated the hell out of him to hear about it from Susan. Being a salesman was like that. You could have booms and busts and you had to ride it out. Something would come up—but in the meantime you had to stay in the game, keep up with your co-workers, and Jeff didn't need any aggravation about it at home when he had enough on his mind during the workday. He could handle all this. He would handle it. And right now, on his way home after slugging it out in the boxing ring, still buzzing along on the coke, he felt so good—so downright punch-drunkenly *great*—that he knew, he just freaking *knew*, that all this would work itself out. It was days like these, it was times like these, that were exactly the reason he liked cocaine in the first place.

The winter sun had set just before 6 P.M. and Jeff pulled his pickup truck into the short driveway that led to his carport, off Berry Tree Drive. He'd made it in time to head inside for dinner with Susan and the kids.

Their single-story light green house with its contrasting dark green trim was by no means large, but it was cozy, and Susan kept it neat, and kept flowers growing in the walled-in front and back yards. The street had a number of tall trees, including several on the Wright property, and Jeff had been undertaking little projects all around the house to make it look better. He'd added lights along the front walkway leading up to the door and he'd just dug out a section of patio on the screened-in porch where he was going to install a fountain.

Jeff liked the whole "Daddy's home!" part of the day, and stepping in from the illuminated pathway that ran across the small front lawn into the bright house with its familiar smells and hubbub was always fun.

Bradley, his 4-year-old son, was constantly impressed with his dad's adventures, and Jeff liked to tell him about boxing. Jeff got a quick kiss and a "How was your day?" from Susan coming in the door, but he also caught a disapproving glance mixed in with the greeting. She knew about the dope, she knew about the cocaine, and although Jeff didn't like to believe it, much less hear about it, Susan seemed to have a knack for spotting the difference in his mood when he was on either. It didn't matter to Jeff. He felt great and he didn't care. If Susan was going to be a sullen bitch about it, then it was her problem. Jeff gave his baby daughter Kaily a kiss and then he went into the other room for a moment to see what Bradley was up to—see if he wanted to mix it up mano a mano with Dad for a moment and do a little playful sparring.

Bradley liked to put up his dukes and play-box with his dad. It got him all worked up, and Jeff thought it was a riot. He'd zap the little guy right back, squirrel around with him, get him laughing. But tonight Bradley was in a petulant mood. Jeff was distracted, and frankly, Bradley wasn't up for the game. Halfheartedly, Bradley punched his dad's open hands as Jeff playfully weaved in front of him. Jeff shot back a right hook and tapped Bradley on the face. Bradley started to snivel and Jeff apologized— but inside it made him mad, because in the tiny house, Susan was going to hear Bradley whine and in a heartbeat be on his case. Susan claimed the cocaine made Jeff too aggressive with the kids. She'd nagged at him in the past about not playing with Bradley when he was high because he played too rough. Now, at the end of a perfectly decent afternoon, Jeff was going to get stuck with another lecture because he'd accidentally connected with Brad in the face.

Jeff was a bit surprised as the moment passed and Susan didn't seem to pick up on it, even though Bradley had worked his way into the kitchen and was grousing to her about how Daddy had punched him. Relaxing on the couch in the front room as the minutes ticked past, Jeff shrugged to himself. If Susan had decided to pass up this opportunity to chew him out, then, after four years of marriage, he must finally be getting through to her.

Sitting in the momentary tranquillity of his home, Jeff didn't realize that Susan had a new strategy for dealing with him being a jerk. She was going to bypass such petty confrontations—and murder him instead.

It was still early evening, but this time of year it was pitch-dark outside and the kids were young enough that they'd already been put to bed.

Thus far, Jeffrey Wright had been having a so-so day and it looked like it was about to wind down as unremarkably as it had begun. Jeff watched a little television and Susan bustled around the kitchen and the bedroom.

Earlier Bradley had been on Jeff's nerves a bit, but he was little and that was no big deal. Jeff really couldn't figure out what Susan was thinking. He was still skating along a bit on the cocaine and not looking forward to coming all the way down off it. In the meantime, Susan seemed almost unusually calm this evening and the thought occurred to him again that maybe they'd turned a corner in their relationship; maybe she was mellowing out a bit and letting him just be himself when he wanted to do his thing and get a little high. He didn't think it needed to be any big deal, and if Susan was prepared to grow up a bit and drop it . . . Jeff looked up and blinked. He'd sort of subconsciously realized that Susan had gone into their small bedroom for a few minutes, but now he was aware that she'd come back. She'd been standing a short distance away looking at him for the past few moments. Her blonde hair was no longer back, it was brushed down over her shoulders and she was leaning languidly against the wall looking at Jeff.

It was too early to be calling it a night, but Susan

was wearing a silk bathrobe and even though the sash was knotted in front, it was draped loosely enough that Jeff could tell she had very little on underneath it. Susan had been a stripper when she was 18, and eight years later she still knew how to look stunning with just a glance and a well-placed hand on her hip. Jeff couldn't help grinning. He knew exactly what that particular glance meant, and his pretty wife was looking pretty good.

Jeff punched off the TV remote and stood up from the davenport. Susan knew that he'd been hooked like a fish, and with a smirk she turned and, letting one hand run slowly along the wall, she sidled back through the open door of the bedroom, giving Jeff a slow, smoldering glance as she disappeared through it.

Still grinning, Jeff followed her into their small, neat bedroom. The lights were off and red candles were softly burning on the dressers and the end tables. Music was playing gently in the background. As the door clicked shut behind him, Susan stepped from the shadows, melted into his arms, and began to kiss him passionately, pausing to undo his shirt, and, more significantly, his belt buckle. He managed to work open the front of her robe and soon he was running his hands along her smooth sides, her soft breasts, her tight rear, smelling her hair and tasting her as they kissed.

Suddenly Susan stopped at the edge of their wood-framed bed. In a playful whisper she suggested that Jeff lay down on their bed.

Jeff was loving this. The coke still buzzing through

his system was making it hard to concentrate on deep thoughts, but he'd never been much of a deep thinker anyway, and this was clearly going to be a very good night.

Susan reached into a bedside drawer and came up with a couple of Jeff's neckties. Leaning over to kiss him again, she took Jeff's outstretched left hand off her breast and expertly looped the necktie around his wrist. With a giggle she quickly fastened the other end of the tie around one of the vertical wooden slats on the headboard of the king-sized bed. Jeff's right hand was working overtime tracing its way around her body, but Susan soon had the other necktie lariated around that wrist as well, and up it went to the opposite corner of the headboard until Jeff's arms were stretched out above him. His attention was entirely focused on Susan at this point; he watched her seductively shrug the robe off her smooth shoulders and let it fall onto the floor. She bent over like the dancer she had been and picked the bathrobe sash up off the floor in one smooth move, giving Jeff a heart-stopping view of her candlelit body in the process. Deftly she tied the sash around his left ankle and once again secured it to the corner post of the bed. Jeff chuckled to himself. This was great! Susan was smiling wickedly at him as she finished attaching another sash to his right ankle and tugging it home into position on the fourth corner of the bed frame.

As Jeff watched his hot little wife sidle her nude body over to the edge of their bed and sling one leg up and over to straddle him, as she sat her nude self confidently down on his naked lap, running her hands up and down his chest, as the candles picked out the blonde highlights in her hair, it occurred again to Jeff that maybe Susan was finally beginning to get the message about who was in charge around here and how he expected to be treated.

He couldn't have been more wrong.

2

Jeff Wright was now naked and tied spread-eagle on the bed. As he gazed up in the flickering candlelight at his nude wife, a look suddenly passed between them that set off a tiny warning bell in the back of Jeff's drug-addled mind. Far from gazing at him with the look of someone who was about to start a smooth ride to ecstasy, Susan seemed to be slowly studying him. More significantly, she seemed to be studying the four connection points where Jeff was anchored to the bed.

Buzzing nervously along on the coke, Jeffrey was turned on and ready to go. This was taking too long. Susan had scooted back off him for a moment and reached for one of the red candles burning beside the bed, but Jeff had seen enough, and impatience was giving way to definite urgency.

Jeff wanted her to hurry, but Susan had already swung back around with the candle in her right hand and she began running her left hand across his chest . . . and lower. "Mmmm," Jeffrey sighed, content that things were once again picking up speed. He could feel her hot breath on his chest as she kissed her way down his skin, and he felt her hand brush over his crotch and down his inner thigh. He took a deeper breath and watched her glance significantly up at him as her hair brushed over his now-erect penis. He smiled greedily, anticipating what would come next, rolling slightly from side to side and wriggling his hips in anticipation as he worked against the twin forces of his growing arousal and the neckties that were holding him fast to the bed frame.

Susan raised her head up and with her left hand she continued to stroke Jeff's thigh. He smiled as he watched the great view of her breasts in the candle-light. Her hand was on his scrotum and he gave an approving sigh of pleasure.

What happened next was anything but pleasant.

Susan glared straight into Jeff's eyes and turned the candle upside down, letting the superheated wax pour right out onto the sensitive skin of his inner thigh. He gave a startled yelp of pain as the burning wax ran down into his crotch. Jeff hissed sharply and protested. But Susan wasn't paying the least bit of attention to what he was saying. In the split second the wax had hit one of Jeff's most sensitive spots, she'd seen something that was critically important demonstrated for her: Jeff had jerked reflexively in an effort to sit up. At any other time the 220-pound amateur boxer wouldn't have had any trouble whatsoever coming to a sitting position, or grabbing her arm, or batting away the dripping candle. But just now Jeff hadn't budged more than a couple of inches in any direction.

Her breath hissed in as adrenaline surged through her, and a burning light came on in her eyes.

Jeff squinted at Susan in the darkness looking for a clue to what was going on. Maybe he was starting to crash down off the cocaine, but suddenly things didn't seem right. In a flash, Susan's moves had gone from languid and seductive to focused and deliberate.

Under the clinical gaze of his wife, Jeff moved rapidly from annoyed to perplexed to slightly alarmed. What Susan had just seen graphically confirmed about Jeff's complete immobility as he lay on the bed was now starting to occur to Jeff as well. It hadn't seemed like an issue at all a couple of minutes ago when Susan was kissing him and playfully tying him up. Right about now he'd have thought he'd be too preoccupied with Susan to care how tightly he was fastened, but instead Susan was looking around the room with a fixed pout. Every trace of seduction was gone out of her face and her slight frame was rigid with purpose. Instead of nude and sexy, Susan now just looked naked and pissed off.

Jeff thrashed his head up for a closer look at what was going on.

Susan had gotten clear off the bed again and she had her back to him as she went rummaging through one of her dresser drawers.

Jeff was just angry and confused. The pain from the hot liquid being poured on his groin had gone and now he could feel the wax hardening on his skin as it cooled. What the hell was Susan's problem? Everything had been going along just fine when she seemed to just flip into an angry mood. Maybe Susan had been pouting because he hadn't reacted like she thought he would to the candle wax move. Maybe this was her idea of a new sex game, and things would pick up again in a minute. Jeff's mind whirred as he tried to figure out what he was looking at. What was she still doing in the dresser? Was this another stupid surprise she'd cooked up in an effort to spice things up? Whatever it was, Jeff wasn't enjoying it anymore and he would have thought Susan would be much more tuned to his likes and dislikes, considering some of the knock-down, drag-out arguments they'd had during their four years of marriage.

Susan slid her shapely ass back onto the bed. She had taken something from the drawer, but in the dim glow from the candles she'd held it out of sight, setting it towards the end of the bed where Jeff couldn't raise his head high enough to see what it was.

There was something about the way Susan was acting that Jeff didn't like. Something was going on behind those pretty eyes that he wasn't used to seeing and that he couldn't figure out. But as the seconds passed, Susan was increasingly her sexy self again.

That thought was blown completely out of Jeff's head as startling, searing, mind-bending pain suddenly shot through his entire body. Something razor sharp had just sliced into his penis. Jeff screamed and strained to sit up, but all he could do was buck his hips up and down.

Wide-eyed, Jeff looked on in horror as he felt Susan grab his injured penis with her left hand and hold up a seven-inch stainless-steel hunting knife with a black riveted handle in her right hand. Jeff was frantically trying to wrap his mind around the concept that Susan had just deliberately cut him in one of the

worst possible ways—and that the knife she was
holding must have been in the dresser the whole evening, and that she must have tied him up for a reason,
and that this was all looking extremely deliberate—
when she brought the knife back down and sliced him
again. Agony blazed up through Jeff's brain. Again
she nicked his penis with the knife.

Susan was yelling now but all Jeff could get was
that his once-meek wife was now remarkably in control of this situation and she seemed to be getting
more wound up to it as the seconds passed.

Jeff had broken out in a cold sweat of fear and
pain, but he was still trying to think how he was going
to get back in control, get Susan off him, get out of
the bedroom, get help, get to a hospital, when Susan
spun around to face him. Still straddling his waist, she
raised the knife back above her head. She was shaking now with rage, but as she watched him strain with
all his might against his bonds, she appeared to be
more and more resolute. Despite the unbelievable
pain and his thrashing, Susan actually seemed to be
emboldened by the blood and the violence. Jeff had
spent four years thinking he was in solid control of
this marriage, but now Susan had the complete upper
hand. Four years of frustration poured out of her, and
as he saw Susan head-on, Jeff began to wonder just
how far she was really going to go with this attack.
Raw dread now flooded through every fiber of Jeff as
his naked wife leaned into his face.

Susan growled, her upper body shivering with
anger. She'd sliced him superficially in his most intimate places, but now Jeff's mind was racing to decide whether she would actually continue to stab him.

He watched wide-eyed as the tip of the blade hovered over his chest and Susan continued her tirade.

Susan hesitated for a second as she set the point of the blade against Jeff's upper chest. He heaved five inches to the side, but the point of the blade moved with him. Susan grimaced watching him struggle, feeling him gyrate between her thighs, and then, squaring her shoulders, and with a whipping action she brought the blade straight up and plunged it right back down into her husband's chest.

From there it just got easier with each hit. Again and again she mechanically hammered the knife up and down into Jeff. Once, twice . . . six, seven, eight times. There was a solid smack as her fist and the knife hilt hit Jeff. With each puncture even more blood began to well up out of him, but Susan just stabbed him again. And again. And again. And again.

She was crying, she was ranting, naming injustice after injustice she'd put up with for four straight years—starting with nervous weeks spent worrying if he was really going to marry her after it was more than clear that she was very pregnant.

The stab wounds were adding up on Jeff and he was writhing in a delirium of pain underneath her, but she simply could no longer care. With each stroke, each dull sticking thud of the knife biting into him, she could feel it bring back a piece of her self-worth that she thought she'd lost forever.

In the candlelight Jeff was now bleeding profusely, but for all the angry red and purple stab wounds, there were still plenty of untouched places, and Susan had four years of abject fear and frustration that she wanted him to atone for at the point of her blade. Susan was on autopilot. The children sleeping down the hall, the neighbors just yards away in every direction, the city and suburbs sprawled around her—all might as well have been light years away.

The knife raised and lowered with the mechanical repetitiveness of the oil derricks scattered throughout Texas. Most of the blows were landing in Jeff's chest but, with her teeth clenched and her grip firmly in place, Susan twisted from side to side and chopped the blade point into every part of him she could reach.

Jeff's face was glazed over in pain and horror now. He'd taken enough drugs in his own lifetime to know what a trip to an alternate reality was like, and Susan had clearly crossed some line and gone someplace else where she was playing by the rules of that universe. He could tell from looking at her that she wasn't going to stop stabbing him. Flecks of blood covered her arms and spattered up onto her breasts. They were on her neck, her face, and in the flying wave of blonde hair that bobbed in time with the blows that just continued to rain down on him.

Jeff had completely lost count, had ceased to care about time. It felt like dozens of hits and with each searing injury, with each agonizing twist of his body, he could feel more blood flowing away and see the candlelight glinting off the steel knife as it traveled upward, blood dripping, to immediately reset itself for the next blazing arc back downward into his body.

Susan kept glancing at the neckties and the sashes holding Jeff in place. They weren't budging. Jeff was fighting a titanic struggle to move anywhere— anywhere out of the range of the blade that kept searching for any point it hadn't already hit—but he knew within moments after Susan began stabbing him that he had no hope. There was nothing he could do, nowhere he could hide. In the instant that she'd first sliced him, he'd already heaved his body as far as it could go in every direction—left, right, backward, forward, up, down. There were no dimensions left—only a searing space of desperation and pain.

Each blow seemed more excruciating than the last until, a scant second later, the blade found some new unmolested spot and tore into it. Susan kept saying things, lots of things, but Jeff's mind was just getting fragments now. She was speaking only a couple feet from him, but that was a world away from his focus on the cutting edge of her knife. She jammed it over and over into this chest until the streaming layer of blood covering it made it difficult to find a new target, so she began plunging it into his neck repeatedly, and then shoving it into his head.

Somewhere in the frenzy, the tip of the blade broke off inside Jeffrey's skull. Somewhere in the madness, the blade drilled straight down through Jeff's eye.

Each stab was a single step in a longer dance, a brushstroke that was part of a larger picture, a means to a climactic end. And then, somewhere in the dark Houston night, that end arrived for Jeff.

Under the hail of flying blood droplets and stainless-steel vindication, somewhere in the midst of the self-righteous adrenaline-soaked fury that was being visited upon him, Jeffrey Wright crossed the line from conscious to unconscious, from viable to unviable—and he died.

It was a profound moment, an important moment,

but it was a moment that Susan Wright missed entirely.

Jeffrey Wright had actually been dead for quite some time when finally, disheveled and exhausted, Susan plunged the knife into his body one final time and then let it fall from her open hand onto the red bedsheets.

3

For a time Susan just sat on the floor near the bed. But then the silence of the house seemed to catch up with her. As the last of the candles began flickering low, she wiped her eyes and tried to figure out what was supposed to happen next.

On the one hand Susan was experiencing a sense of almost supernatural horror over what she had just done with a ten-dollar hunting knife. But on the other hand there was the feeling that something long overdue had finally taken place and that the universe was putting right something that had been terribly wrong.

Jeff-the-Problem was over. All the things that she'd had to alter and suppress and manage and track and think about because of Jeff and his violent control-freak tendencies were now gone, because Jeff was gone. A huge weight had been lifted from her. There would be no more hellacious arguments, no tough ultimatums leading to a bitter divorce, no protracted custody battle, no trading the kids up every other weekend. Jeff was just no more, finished, gone. Problem solved.

But in the lingering candlelight of the small bedroom on Berry Tree Drive, another realization was creeping in just as fast. Jeff and all his mind-crushing prerogatives, prejudices, and pressures may have been gone from her life, but his big heavy dead body was still tied down to the center of their bed. Susan began to feel cold and realized that it was because her naked body had been spritzed with a mist of Jeff's blood droplets, which were starting to dry on her skin.

Susan knew she had to think. Before she'd met Jeff, when she still thought of herself as a competent young woman, she had done her own thinking. She'd even dared to think of herself as spunky and independent. She'd been a Brownie, she'd been a cheerleader, she'd been a church youth group leader, she'd even been an 18-year-old topless dancer strutting down a bar in her birthday suit making grown men drool. She could handle things. She could take care of herself. She could figure this out.

The first thing was to get some clothes on. Susan cast about the darkened floor looking for the sash to her bathrobe before realizing that it was still secured firmly around Jeff's ankle. She glanced back at the bed. The candles were just about out now and in the oppressive dark, Jeff's extremely still form had sort of a menacing quality to it. Steeling herself, Susan walked over to the doorway and flicked on the light switch.

The surge of pure white light into the room made Susan catch her breath. Under the stark glare of electric lights, the room looked like what it was: an astonishingly gory crime scene.

Everywhere Susan looked there were droplets of bright red blood. Everywhere. The bed, the sheets, the bedspread, the walls, the floor, the furniture, even the ceiling were suffused with blood droplets that had been thrown out in arcs over and over and over in every direction by the pendulum swings of her knife. Additional pints of it had seeped out of Jeffrey and run down into the mattress, box spring, and carpet like a special effect in a high-school haunted house attraction. And topping it all off was what was left of Jeff.

This wasn't good. Susan had to get a grip. She had to sort it out. She realized the first thing was to get a shower and get herself dressed, in case she had to deal with the children, who so far had slept through the whole thing, but who couldn't be allowed to see her splashed from head to foot in blood.

Padding quietly down the hallway, Susan made her way into the bathroom and turned on the shower. She let the water run and run, and in the stark light she could see the blood swirling away down the drain. Back in the bedroom Susan quickly threw on some clothing.

Emotions were beginning to overwhelm her. This had all seemed a lot simpler when she was hiding the knife and lighting the candles, but now she desperately wanted to talk to someone. She wanted to talk about Jeff. Jeff was the reason for all this. He had made her do this. Jeff might be dead, but she was still angered beyond belief by what he had put her through for the past four years in the name of nothing more complicated than a normal marriage.

Susan couldn't call her mother, because she also

lived in Houston. If her mom became sufficiently alarmed, there was a chance she would drive over to the house to talk to Susan in person. The same problem was going to present itself if she called her younger sister Cindy. Cindy was a psychologist, and she'd helped on other occasions when she and Jeff were having problems, but Susan couldn't risk Cindy coming over. That only left her in-laws in Austin, which was conveniently 150 miles away. Susan picked up the phone and placed a call to the Wrights.

Ron and Kay Wright were shocked by what their distraught daughter-in-law was telling them. Susan began by describing Jeff returning in a rage that evening from boxing lessons and throwing a violent tantrum. During the course of it, he'd hit Bradley in the face and roughed her up as well. When they asked to speak to Jeff, Susan said they couldn't, because he had taken off. When they wondered how long he'd be gone, Susan said that she thought he'd left her and the kids for good.

The Wrights were stunned. They had seen their son and daughter-in-law and their two young grandchildren practically every other week since Jeff and Susan got married. They'd known about some ups and downs in the marriage, but they had no reason to suspect it was on the rocks. It had been the holidays, only two weeks before, when they had all gotten together last, and Jeff seemed fine. Now Susan was telling them that he'd hit her and hit Bradley and stormed off while raving about never coming back. Why, the Wrights wondered, would Jeff do such a thing?

Susan had a short answer for them: drugs. Susan said flat-out that Jeff had been taking drugs for some time, and it had now become a severe habit. Furthermore, Jeff had been missing work because of it. He had also been running into debt and he'd tried to borrow several thousand dollars from friends to catch up on his payments for cocaine. This was all horrifying news to the Wrights. Jeff's father knew that his son had had a drug problem in the past, but was under the impression it had long since been brought under control. None of this sounded like the Jeff they had raised, and as this was being dumped on them in the middle of the night, they really didn't know what to do or say.

Susan spoke to the Wrights for over an hour, thoroughly upsetting them in the process. They were concerned about her, they were concerned about their grandchildren, but they especially wanted to get hold of Jeffrey and see what was going on, see if they could help, see if they could get him back to his senses. Susan was evasive. She had no idea where Jeff had gone or where he might turn up. Her best suggestion was just to wait until morning and call him at his office.

Finally the call ended. However cathartic it had been to tell somebody else what a jerk Jeff had really been in recent months, she was right back with the same predicament she'd faced when she picked up the phone. Jeff's body was still where she had left it, and now she'd tipped off other people that Jeff was unaccounted for—that he needed to be found.

The Wrights would spend a sleepless night in Austin thinking of ways to get in touch with Jeff and figure out what was really going on. Susan would spend the rest of the night awake in Houston trying to make sure that no one would ever find out.

During the four years of their marriage Susan had worried constantly about where Jeff was and what he was up to; now she had a different and much more serious problem on her hands. She had to get him out of the bedroom, but then what? Jeff weighed 220 pounds. She couldn't just put him out in a trash can. In theory there were a lot of places to dump a body in the 8,700 square miles that make up greater Houston—not to mention the thirteen scenic bayous winding through it—but she couldn't just stuff him in a vehicle and drive off in the middle of the night, leaving the kids behind. What if something happened? There were houses packed in tightly around her on Berry Tree Drive and plenty of cars driving past even after dark. What if the neighbors saw her out in the driveway struggling with a large object wrapped in a bloody sheet?

Walking out onto the screened-in patio behind the carport, Susan took a look at a shallow hole Jeff had recently dug. It was one of his little home-improvement projects. He had been planning to install a fountain with a small pump buried underneath. The kids would like it and it would give the empty concrete patio some badly needed character.

Jeff had cut away a three-foot-wide slice of the concrete patio slab, then dug a trench in the dirt underneath. The hole was right alongside the wall of the bedroom where his body now lay tied to the bedposts. The whole thing wasn't very deep, but it was big enough to hold a person—and it was all Susan had to work with. Looking at the hole, Susan decided that she could bury Jeff here.

Back in the bedroom Susan was forced to take a good look at her husband. It was awful. She had stabbed Jeff a lot. Dozens and dozens of times, from the look of it. His face and upper torso were practically obliterated by the ferocity of the attack. The passing hours caused Jeff's wounds and all the dried blood to do worse and worse things to his already tortured appearance.

The neckties and the sashes were still solidly in place. They were stiff with dried blood, and after a moment, Susan gave up trying to untie them. Casting about, she got hold of the knife and swiftly cut through each one. Now she just had to get Jeff from Point A to Point B. Touching him tentatively, she steeled herself for what had to happen next. Grimacing, she pulled him off the bed. He hit the floor with a definite thud. He was much heavier and a bit stiffer than she had expected. There's a reason for the expression "dead weight," and Susan was starting to see what a chore it would be to get Jeff down the hallway, through the house, and out to a hole that was just on the other side of the bedroom wall.

Susan tried to get a hold of Jeff under his armpits, but the proximity to his battered head and destroyed face, and the staggering amount of blood on his upper torso, made her change her mind. Instead, she grabbed him by his ankles and began to move him. It was hard going. She didn't want to make any noise that would wake the children. Susan slowly dragged Jeff's naked corpse through the dark and silent house. Inch by inch, pull by pull, she worked the body towards the undignified resting place that awaited it. Jeff slid on his back, leaving a swath of blood down the hallway and across the concrete patio.

Ready or not, it was time to bury Jeff. Susan tried for a few minutes to enlarge the grave that Jeff had unknowingly dug for himself, but she didn't make much progress. It was getting very late. She was exhausted. The upper sections of the porch were screened, but they were open to the elements and it was possible that someone could hear her if she went at it with a shovel in the middle of the night. She just wanted this awful task done with as soon as possible.

Susan dragged, shoved, and pushed Jeff's bloodied form into the ground. The sensation of tucking him into the cramped space as his limbs stiffened was beyond weird. Finally, he was in as far as he was going to go, bent forward in a kind of crumpled, seated pose. Susan let his head flop face down on his knees and began to scoop the pile of dirt back over him. This task went a lot more quickly than she had expected and as she smoothed the last of the dirt level with the patio, she realized to her dismay that Jeff wasn't buried very far down at all. If six feet under was some sort of standard, then frankly, she wasn't convinced he was all of six inches under right now. Susan didn't even want to have to think what this meant. Jeff was out of sight, for the moment at least. It would have to do for now.

The sun would be coming up soon. The kids would be waking up and looking for breakfast. It was about to be a new day in a fundamentally altered world, and these sorts of morbid problems could wait.

Susan got out a roll of paper towels and began retracing her steps from the patio back to the bedroom looking for dabs of blood. There would be time to clean up the bedroom as Tuesday wore on, and after that she would figure out how she and the children were going to go on with their new lives. As painful and as dreadful as this cathartic night had been, it was almost over. She had done the worst of it. Now she just had to get away with it.

4

Tuesday dawned with its own set of problems.

Jeff was at least momentarily out of the way under the patio, but daylight brought home the full immensity of the task Susan would face when it came to wiping up the bedroom.

This was not just some tough household cleaning job. It was going to be up there with remodeling after a flood or hurricane.

One glance at the bed and it was obvious someone had been murdered on it. The blood had saturated the sheets, bedspread, mattress, and box spring. They were beyond cleaning. She was simply going to have to find a way to get rid of those items.

Susan stripped off the sheets and bundled them into a trash bag. Checking that the kids were occupied, she took a wheeled gray metal dolly Jeff had purchased and hauled the blood-soaked mattress out to the back yard. Next she lugged out the box spring, and, after struggling to pull it apart into its component pieces, the wooden bed frame followed. It was a start, but it wasn't much of one.

Susan knew she had to figure out a way to get rid of the mattress and box spring, but even though she could use Jeff's pickup truck, this was a real problem. It's always a pain to dispose of something as large as an old mattress, but she couldn't take this one to a landfill, because when anyone took a look at it, the bloodstains were going to raise immediate questions.

The same problem was going to loom if she tossed the mattress into a vacant lot or one of the many bayous that ran through Houston. Weeks might pass, but whenever someone did stumble upon these bulky items, the odds were they were going to spot the enormous stains, recognize them as blood, and call the police.

The bed was just too much of a puzzle. For the moment Susan decided to leave it in the back yard and concentrate her efforts on the inside of the house.

With the bed removed it became clear that the bedroom carpet had soaked up another large pool of blood that had dripped off the bed frame as Jeff lay dying, and now that huge stain would have to be dealt with as well.

After a few attempts at scrubbing the blood off the walls, Susan realized it would actually be faster and more effective to just paint over it. Next, she went down the hall, grabbed a bottle of bleach from the laundry, and returned to start in on the carpet. She used up the whole bottle on the big bloody spot. It made some difference, but not enough. She'd need to buy more bleach when she got the paint.

The whole time Susan was preoccupied with trying to make a crime scene disappear, she still had two children and a dog to keep busy. The dog, with its sensitive nose, had become very interested in the patio area where Jeff was buried. That simply terrified Susan. If the dog could already smell Jeff's body less than a day after he had been killed, then how long was it going to take before people could smell it as well?

The only fix she could think of would be to bury the body even deeper, but there was no time for that. Besides, if she was going to deepen the fountain pit, that would mean that first she would have to disinter Jeff and set him out of the way on the concrete while she worked—not something she was prepared to contemplate, let alone do.

Susan reasoned that if she could put more dirt on top of Jeff, then it would be pretty much the same thing as burying him deeper. There had to be a certain point at which the depth of the soil on top of the body would hide the scent from the dog.

Susan piled the kids into the pickup truck and made a couple of stops. The first was at the office of her doctor, who had treated her since she was a teenager. She had some surface cuts on the back of her right hand checked. Then it was time for a brief run to the mall. She quickly bought paint and paint rollers, several more jugs of bleach, and ten bags of garden topsoil.

Back at the house the phone was already ringing. It was Kevin Conboy, Jeff's supervisor at the carpet factory, wondering why Jeff hadn't shown up for work.

Susan took a deep breath and then matter-of-factly explained that Jeff had come home drunk the night before. He had hit Bradley, so she had thrown him out of the house. She had no idea where he had gone.

Conboy was surprised. Susan seemed calm, but Conboy was increasingly concerned as he tried to figure out what this meant was going to happen to a key employee. Susan volunteered that Jeff was having financial problems and said she thought that was a factor in his behavior.

Jeff's parents had also had a sleepless night. When they called back during the day wondering if Jeff had returned, Susan said that, as a matter of fact, he had come back. She told the Wrights that Jeff had stormed back in mid-day, angry as ever, on a mission to collect his clothing, and that once again he'd gotten into a shouting match with her. Jeff was so out of control that he'd grabbed a bottle of bleach from the laundry area and shaken it all over the bedroom and her clothes as he yelled at her. This new episode baffled the Wrights. They didn't think it sounded like Jeff at all, and now, more than ever, they wanted to be able to talk to their son, to try to get some idea of what was upsetting him. But once again, Susan said she had no idea where he'd stomped off to, and, once again, she said that Jeff had managed to forget to take his cell phone with him.

A short time later Susan told the same story all over again to her close friend and neighbor Jamie Darr-Hall. Darr-Hall was upset by the tale. She'd had reason in the past to suspect that Susan might be the victim of abuse, so she told her to call the police and file a report. She also urged Susan to change the locks on the house.

By the time she had gotten everybody off the phone and out of her hair, Susan was exhausted. She'd been up all night and most of the day with very little time to stop and think. Jeff had been dead less than twenty-four hours, but already things were piling up on her. People were calling, very concerned people, and they were asking increasingly difficult questions. Susan knew she only had a few days, really maybe just a few hours, to get everything back under control.

On Wednesday, Susan bundled Bradley and Kaily back into her car and headed out on a nine-mile trip to a police station on Cypresswood Drive in the neighboring municipality of Spring.

Susan walked through the door of the Harris County Precinct 4 constable's office wearing jeans and a red sweater saying that she wanted to report a case of domestic abuse and request a restraining order against her husband.

Susan's story was straightforward and mirrored a pattern the deputies had heard time and again when it came to spousal abuse. Susan said she had been willing to put up with escalating belittlement and beatings during her four years of marriage, but now, since her husband had begun hitting her oldest child, she was no longer going to sit by and let this continue.

Family violence happened to be the number one cause of injury to women in Harris County, as it is in hundreds of other counties nationwide. So the fact that Susan was standing at the counter with two young children in tow saying that her husband had gone off the deep end was something the staff had a great deal of experience handling.

Susan was shown in to speak with Deputy Constable Scott Hall of the Family Violence Unit, who took a close look at the nicks and a couple of pronounced cuts on Susan's right hand and wrist as well as some dark bruises on her arms and legs.

Susan looked sincere. A well-groomed 26-year-old with two young children, determined to stop a cycle of abuse, but at the same time worried sick about what was going to happen when her violent husband found out she was talking to police, all seemed plausible and truthful.

The injuries were minor and Bradley didn't show any signs of severe abuse, but Deputy Hall noted Susan's extreme fear and set about having her injuries photographed.

Kaily was clearly too young to be of any help, but an investigator from Harris County's Children's Protective Services took Bradley into a playroom at the office. They began by getting him some color crayons and paper. Then a video camera was turned on and Bradley was quizzed about what had been going on at his home.

The investigator led Bradley through a series of questions designed to stress to him the differences between lies and the truth before the questioning turned to his parents' relationship. Bradley said he couldn't think of any times when he'd seen his father hit his mother, but for four nights in a row he could remember his father coming home and "punching" him. Bradley said that he hadn't done anything wrong to deserve being hit.

When it was her turn to be interviewed, Susan gave an account of Monday night that began with Jeff coming home in a rage and then storming out after he'd hit her and Bradley. She broke down and cried several times during the next three hours.

Susan had visible injuries and a consistent story, and looked for all the world like a responsible wife and mother. The deputies filled out the paperwork and swore out arrest warrants for Jeffrey Wright on two counts—assault on a family member and injury to a child. They were prepared to send a cruiser straight out to wherever Jeff was and arrest him. So where, deputies asked, could they find him? Susan didn't know. She hadn't seen him since he'd stormed out of the house in a rage two nights before.

Jeff's description was circulated to police officers in the precinct and he was entered into their computer system as a wanted person. Once police did come across Jeff, they would slap him in handcuffs.

Susan had done what she came to do. She was ready to return home, but as far as the police were concerned, this was the beginning rather than the end of the process. In a normal domestic violence case the police expected that at a minimum there would be counseling for both parties, a scheduled trial or plea bargain on the criminal charges, and, in all likelihood, an eventual divorce.

Deputy Hall asked Susan point blank why she hadn't already filed for a divorce. Susan muttered something about how divorce didn't seem like a very Christian thing to do. Hall shrugged it off. Most abused women don't have any great-sounding reason why they let somebody pound on them again and again.

Hall took Susan over to another office and introduced her to the Victim's Assistance liaison. Susan may or may not have felt that she was a victim, but Harris County certainly did, and it was standard procedure to get women who came in reporting abuse right on track to receive counseling and assistance geared to getting them out of the mess they were in.

If every woman who got hit in this country simply stood up on the spot, gathered up any kids, and permanently left the person who'd hit them, there wouldn't really be much concern with a "cycle of violence and abuse." However, grim experience has shown that women will stay . . . and stay . . . and stay with someone who hurts them, even in horrific ways. The psychology of abusers and the abused often provides its own fuel in the form of a victim who allows mistreatment to continue even though she realizes it's ruining her life.

Women who are abused often want to minimize the severity of their situation or pass their individual cases off as "not that bad," but officials who see the same thing week in and week out have learned not to take such excuses lightly. When Susan was ushered in to see the Victim's Assistance liaison, she was strongly urged to fill out the paperwork that would get her the help she needed. Susan insisted that there was no need for her to check into a battered women's shelter, but the county was also prepared to help her through its Crime Victim's Compensation program, and the liaison gave her the forms and helped her fill one out. The liaison explained that Susan was potentially eligible for help with everything from the cost of her medical expenses, to counseling, legal fees, and any other reasonable financial burdens that could arise as the result of her and the children being assaulted. Standing there reporting that her husband had just beaten her and her son two days before, Susan had little choice but to fill out the paperwork that logically came with that circumstance.

Back at Jeff's office, things were becoming increasingly difficult for his supervisor Kevin Conboy. It was mid-week and Jeff's phone was ringing off the hook: customers demanded to know what was going to happen to their orders. Conboy got in his car and decided to head out to find Jeff. He checked a number of spots Jeff frequented, but no one had seen him. Finally, on a hunch, Conboy took a drive down to White Oak Bend. Jeff's pickup was in the driveway, but when Conboy rang the doorbell, no one answered. He checked around the house, but all was quiet. Frustrated and baffled, Conboy drove back to work.

On Thursday, Susan was back on the phone with the Wrights. Jeff's parents were frantic. It had been over seventy-two hours since anyone other than Susan had seen or spoken to him. They couldn't make sense of his actions. Why would he take off without so much as his cell phone, let alone his pickup truck? What, they wondered, was Susan doing about it all? Susan told them that she had mainly been trying to clean up the bedroom because of the bleach Jeff had dumped over everything, but she couldn't get rid of the caustic smell, so she'd gotten rid of the mattress and was in the process of tearing up the carpet.

Kevin Conboy was having his third bad day in a row at the office. Jeff still hadn't called in. When he called the Wrights' house, Susan had changed the outgoing message on the answering machine and removed Jeff's voice from the tape. When Conboy talked to Susan, it sounded more and more like her marriage with Jeff was over. Conboy thought this episode had the look of something that was going to turn into a nasty divorce just as soon as Jeff resurfaced.

Conboy was wrestling with what he should do when the Harris County Sheriff's Department called and asked how they could locate Jeff. They had warrants for his arrest. Conboy had heard enough. He made the decision that Jeff was now fired. As soon as Jeff did call in to the company, he would be told not to bother coming back.

On Friday, Deputy Constable Hall called Susan again to tell her that the court had granted her request for a restraining order. Hall said the police were all set to serve it on Jeff, but they still couldn't find him. Susan didn't have any new information beyond the fact that Jeff had left his cell phone at the house, so she suggested they keep checking out his workplace.

When the sun came up on Saturday, Susan was right at the breaking point. The kids were very young and couldn't tell what was amiss, but they had a routine that was increasingly disrupted. Susan could keep them out of her bedroom while she cleaned and cleaned, but they also had to stay off the patio and out of the back yard.

Relatives, co-workers, friends, neighbors, and police were calling constantly looking for any word of Jeff's whereabouts, promising their support, offering to come over and comfort her—which was the last thing she needed. The bedroom was still a bloody mess, but so far Susan, the wife of a carpet salesman, had only managed to get half of the carpet cut away. There were paint cans and cleaning products all over the house and a pile of bloodstained junk that used to be their bed in the back yard. One walk through the place and it would just scream "Murder!" There was just no way to miss what had happened.

Susan was now feeling pressure from everyone. Serious questions were being asked and she couldn't think of answers. Out of this entire surreal week, stabbing Jeffrey to death had been, it was becoming clear, the easiest part of it. Cleaning away the evidence in order to get Jeff completely out of her life had proven to be overwhelming.

The damn dog was the final straw. Susan had been locked for hours in her bedroom trying to cover the traces, stain by stain, drop by drop. She could keep an eye on two kids, two families, an office full of bewildered co-workers, and an entire precinct of constables who were on the hunt for her husband, but she couldn't do all of that and still keep ahead of one chow-mix dog at the same time. Now, after five days of trying, the dog had somehow gotten itself out onto the patio and—to Susan's abject horror—it had begun digging up something that it smelled in the soil below.

The thin layer of potting soil that Susan had spread over the corpse was now scattered around the patio. The dog had begun running around with each of the objects it had excavated from the shallow hole. A dirt-covered bathrobe sash had been dragged out into the back yard. A bloodstained hunting knife was sitting a few feet from the fountain hole.

And so was one other terrifying item.

Jeff's corpse was now partially unearthed. His left shoulder was completely exposed and his stiff arm reached forward as though he were trying to grab the edge of the concrete slab in order to pull himself the rest of the way out. Just visible beneath the arm was the back of Jeff's head where the dog had been scraping away at the dirt. In a final, horrible indignity, Jeff's left hand was out on the patio a few feet from the body. The dog had chewed it off as it worked to tug its former master up from his hastily constructed grave.

Susan took one look and that was it.

She couldn't go on another day like this. She was in way beyond where she could handle things and she had to have help.

Once again Susan put the kids in her car. But this time she headed over to see her mother, Susan Wyche, who had spent the week on the phone trying to comfort her daughter. Wyche didn't think much of her son-in-law. She thought Jeffrey was violent and she knew that from early on in the relationship, Susan had lived in fear of him, but the simple fact was, Wyche really didn't know what to do about it. If her daughter's marriage had now come to a point where it really was going to disintegrate, then there were parts of that scenario that actually came as a relief to Wyche. Lots of couples got divorces. It wasn't the end of the world, no matter how upsetting it might seem at the time. But Wyche couldn't get a straight answer out of Susan about what had happened.

Over in Austin, the Wrights hadn't just been calling Susan in their search for Jeff. They'd also talked with Wyche and, after they compared what Susan had been telling her mother against what Susan had been telling them, they sensed that Susan's version of events didn't add up.

Five days after this apparent marital meltdown, there was one significant point that everyone else was noticing, but that Susan didn't seem to be overly concerned about: namely that Jeff hadn't just walked out on his wife and kids—it was more like he had disappeared off the face of the Earth. Susan's story about Jeff stomping out on Monday night and then returning Tuesday morning for his clothes, without bothering to take either his pickup truck or his cell phone, made no sense to anyone.

Speaking to her mother on Saturday, Susan had talked about restraining orders, and cleaning up the house, and worrying that Jeff would kill her, and—like so much else this alarming week—it wasn't making any real sense to Wyche.

Finally Susan said flat-out that "something awful" had happened, and she was afraid that when Jeff found out, he would return and kill her. Wyche looked closely at her daughter and asked the question that was bothering her: "Susan, did you kill Jeff?" Susan slumped forward with a nod and put her head on the table.

It was actually not the answer Wyche had expected.

"Oh," Wyche replied, at a complete loss for words.

This was far beyond what Wyche had thought she would have to handle this weekend. She paused and began to think of a plan. Susan clearly needed legal help, and with Jeff dead and gone there was also the matter of Wyche's two young grandchildren.

Wyche suggested the kids go spend some time with Susan's sister, Cindy, who had a doctorate in child psychology, and that Susan meet up with a lawyer as quickly as possible back at her house. It was a Saturday, but Wyche had contacts with the prestigious Houston law firm of DeGuerin Dickson & Hennessy, and she would stress that this was an emergency.

Susan, completely beaten by the events of the past week, agreed this was the best course of action.

With that, mother and grandmother took Bradley and Kaily to Target to do some quick shopping and then to Burger King for lunch before Susan headed back home to Berry Tree Drive to await the arrival of a lawyer.

It was time to tell the world where Jeff really was.

5

Attorney Neal Davis had gotten a cryptic message from his law firm that he needed to help out a client's daughter in Northwest Houston. Furthermore, he needed to do it right now, even though it was the middle of the weekend and lawyers have never been known for making house calls.

The details were sketchy—something about a husband and wife having one hell of a fight and the husband now being missing. Davis didn't know exactly what to expect, but he did know that the woman's mother was describing this as a life-and-death emergency.

Although the firm he worked for had represented a veritable who's-who of high-profile Texas defendants, including David Koresh, the 31-year-old Davis was a relatively new arrival. He'd graduated magna cum laude from the University of Southern California and gone on to law school at the University of Texas, but he had not yet been out-front on any high-profile Houston cases. That was about to change in a matter of minutes.

Davis arrived at 10822 Berry Tree Drive mid-afternoon and strode up the short walkway to the front door. It looked like a normal well-kept house on an ordinary side street. He was greeted at the door by a pretty blonde 26-year-old woman who looked like she'd been crying.

Susan was welcoming but skittish. It was an awkward conversation at first, but as they sat in the front room, she began telling Davis about her husband and her life for the four years that she'd been married to him. She told him about the good things—especially their two young children—but she also said there were real problems.

Susan said Jeff was extremely controlling. He could be violent. Jeff was a perfectionist—at least he was when it came to critiquing Susan's efforts. She wasn't so convinced that he was as meticulous when it came to his own habits.

Susan told Davis that Jeff had developed a running interest in dope, particularly coke, and now the cost of those drugs had become unmanageable. He'd tried to beg and borrow money to cover financial shortfalls and the ongoing money problems were in turn causing him to use more drugs.

Susan knew that Jeff and his friends liked to drop in at Houston's topless bars and admire the scenery, but she suspected that he was doing a lot more than just looking when it came to other women. She had been getting phone calls at the house from women whom he had apparently been having affairs with. He'd spent a weekend at a sales conference in Vegas and managed to come back and give her herpes in the bargain—something she doubted he'd gotten playing blackjack.

To add insult to injury, it was Jeff who was obsessed with the notion that Susan might be having affairs when she was out of his sight. Whenever she left the house, he wanted to know where she was going and how long she was staying. He had crazy ideas about just who she could be seeing and when. He called her constantly on her cell phone to ask her where she was and who she was with. If he thought she took too long getting groceries, he accused her of having affairs with the bag boys at the supermarket.

Davis was sympathetic, but this all sounded like the prelude to a divorce case, albeit one with a domestic abuse component. In the grand scheme of the law this was pretty routine stuff, not something you drag a high-priced attorney out on the weekend to listen to on an emergency basis.

As Susan talked and cried she constantly referred to Jeff in the present tense and seemed most concerned about a horrific fight she and Jeff had had just five days before.

Susan said she had been home taking care of the kids when Jeff arrived from a late afternoon boxing lesson high on cocaine. He'd mixed it up with Bradley in a little father–son play-boxing, but when Bradley didn't want to engage in it, Jeff had become angry and struck the 4-year-old in the face. She said that when she objected and put the upset boy to bed, Jeff had turned his attention, and his rage, on her.

Through tears, Susan said that Jeff had shoved her into the bedroom and forced her to have sex with him. Afterwards, hurt and upset herself, she had decided that enough was enough. She began crying and saying that this had gone too far and that Jeff had to get help for his drug habit, which was now spinning out of control and threatening his family and his financial future. Jeff had become enraged. Still high on the cocaine, he was in no mood for some sort of intervention in his own home, in his own bedroom, from his own wife.

As Susan explained it to Davis, she was still lying on the bed sniffling with her eyes closed when she suddenly heard the words "Die, bitch!"

She snapped open her eyes to see Jeff standing right above her with his arm raised and a stainless-steel hunting knife gripped in his hand, about to plunge it straight down into her. The tale was pouring out of Susan as she sat and wiped away tears, and Davis listened raptly.

In an instant Susan had felt that this was it. She was going to die. Right in her own bed at the age of 26 with two young children just down the hallway, it was going to be the end of the road for her, right here on Berry Tree Drive. Suddenly, Susan said, she made a snap decision to fight back, really fight back, for the first time in her marriage to Jeff. She lunged up off the bed and grabbed for the knife. Startled by his normally passive wife's surprise move, and still under the influence of the cocaine, Jeff hesitated for a split second. That was all Susan needed to get a grip on the knife. As the two of them collapsed down onto the bed, she stabbed Jeff with all her might.

With the die cast, and fearing that it would only be a split second before Jeff regained control and turned the tables to kill her, Susan stabbed him again. And then again, and again, and again in rapid succession. In the flurry of stabs and the raging struggle on the bed the outcome never occurred to Susan during those first frenzied moments—but as each plunge of the blade made it into Jeff's body the odds began to change. Within moments Susan was winning and Jeffrey was losing.

Once Susan gained the upper hand, she never let up. Standing over Jeff's supine form on the bed as he tossed in agony, Susan found she just couldn't stop stabbing him. The dam had burst on four years of suppressed anger and spousal oppression and the wave of vengeance just poured out of her. She kept stabbing Jeff as hard as she could, over and over again.

The story was disjointed and Susan was crying, so Davis was having some difficulty tracking all the details. As the moments ticked by, it sounded to him as though Susan was describing a fatal encounter. After all, she was the one sitting here on the davenport telling the story, and Jeff was nowhere to be seen. However, what was really disconcerting was that Susan kept glancing around the house and talking in conspiratorial tones, as if Jeff was going to come howling through the door with an ax at any moment and attack Susan all over again.

Davis wanted to know where Jeff had gone after having been stabbed so many times. Had he gotten to a hospital? Was he dead? Susan was confused about that. She talked about reporting him missing and she also talked about putting him on the patio and pouring dirt on him. She kept saying that when he "woke up," he was going to be tremendously angry and come back and hurt her and the kids.

Susan described spending a week trying to clean up the messy bedroom so that Jeff wouldn't be angry when he saw it—and at the same time she had been sitting up nights bolt-awake on this very couch clutching a knife, terrified that Jeff would return at any moment and attack her.

As he listened to Susan "explain" what had been going on in the house the past five days, Davis became more and more worried. He knew the implications of some of the things she was describing, but he wanted her to show him what she was talking about.

Susan walked him through the house to the patio and opened the door. After just a moment's observation, the blood drained right out of Davis' face. There was a peculiar smell in the air, and at the edge of the patio, right up against the side of the house, there was what looked like an arm, an arm that no longer ended in a hand, reaching up from a ghastly form that was hunched just out of sight beneath the dirt.

This situation wasn't exactly covered in most law school textbooks. Davis was standing in a house in broad daylight next to a woman who was asking for his legal help—who was in fact now his client—and she'd just told him that she'd stabbed her husband to death, and led him to the body. Yet she seemed to think her husband was, in some sense, alive. Beyond the legal complexities involved, Davis was also standing in a room with a psychologically unbalanced woman who'd obviously killed someone a few days before and who was making no real sense.

Davis was now right smack in the middle of an undiscovered crime scene and he needed to sort out several legal and practical issues right away. Susan had already told him that her children were with their grandmother on their way to her sister's, so that was one major problem covered. Davis had a moral duty to call the cops as soon as possible, but as a defense attorney, he also had an ethical duty to do the right thing by Susan. After all, the only reason he was standing here on Berry Tree Drive embroiled in this mess was that he had specifically been called in to help her.

It occurred to Davis that if he just picked up the phone and called 911, the police would come blazing out to the scene and immediately take Susan into custody as a murder suspect. It looked to Davis like Susan was in no position to undergo a police interrogation, and it was his responsibility to keep her legal position intact if and when all this went to trial.

Davis could tell that Susan was under tremendous stress—stress right up to and over the breaking point—and, from her statements about Jeff still being a threat, he had enormous doubts about her mental condition. It seemed obvious that he would need to get her some kind of psychiatric care immediately. Davis made a decision. Jeff's body had been in the ground for almost five full days now. It could wait there a few hours longer.

Susan gathered up a few things and got into Davis' car. He put in a few phone calls and drove her right to the NeuroPsychiatric Center ward of the Texas Medical Center, not far from the Houston Astrodome. He gave her what instructions he could about keeping quiet and told her not to disclose anything about her case to investigators without him being present. He would talk to the police, he would tell them about the killing, and he would be there when detectives eventually interviewed her. Even though she had killed

Jeff, Susan had a legal right to all these protections, and Davis was determined to see that they were preserved and respected.

He'd done his primary duty as far as his client was immediately concerned. Now it was time to kick the police investigation into motion.

6

Police deal with crime and mayhem at the street level. Attorneys deal with it in courtrooms and offices. So when it came to reporting Jeff's death, Davis drove downtown to the Harris County justice complex to speak to the prosecutors working the Intake Division.

Several hours had passed since he'd been sent to Susan Wright's home, but, as Saturday afternoon turned to evening and the winter sun sank over the horizon, the horror of what he had seen on the patio still preyed on Davis' nerves.

Davis trembled as he walked through the front doors of the towering Harris County Criminal Justice Center on Franklin Street. The staff who'd pulled weekend duty at the office knew immediately that something was wrong just by looking at him. His hands shook as he turned over a business card from his prestigious law firm, then struggled to write Susan's Berry Tree Drive address on the back of it.

Davis stammered that he was a lawyer who had to relay an important message on behalf of a client. Furthermore, because of attorney–client privilege, Davis said, he couldn't tell the authorities whom he was representing. Handing his card to Assistant District Attorney Terese Buess, Davis paused and then dropped his bombshell. "There's a dead body at this address and I can't say anything else."

It didn't take long for the first patrol cars, and then the detectives, to converge on what until minutes before had been a quiet side street.

The officers let themselves in through the wooden gate and started by knocking on the front door. When they didn't get an answer they walked around the sides of the darkened house to see if they could spot anything amiss. In the narrow space between a neighbor's brick wall and the enclosed porch, they were able to see through the screens. With the aid of flashlights they could see a patch of dirt at the edge of the patio and something that looked very much like a dead body sticking up from the soil.

As the evening progressed and investigators got into the house, they quickly found the body, the bloody bedroom, the junked mattress in the back yard, and a stack of unopened bags of potting soil stacked in the back of the pickup truck.

In short order police made the connection between their being at the Wright residence and the fact that Jeffrey Wright had been reported as a missing person and the suspect in an alleged case of domestic abuse.

Detectives immediately developed a working theory that they were looking at the corpse of Jeffrey Wright and that he'd been killed on or near the blood-soaked bed. Those facts meant that Susan Wright was a logical suspect. But, for the moment, detectives had to take things step by step. The condition of the body, even after less than a week in the ground, meant that a positive identification of the remains would require the medical examiner.

As the authorities worked into the night, there were three main areas of interest. The most obvious was the patio. There, the way Susan had dropped Jeffrey down into an almost seated position, combined with the dog's digging, had produced a macabre tableau vivant which made it look like Jeff was straining to pull himself out of the hole. In a flowerpot just a few feet from the body was a curvy knife that was missing the pointed tip. It appeared to be covered in dried blood.

The second area of interest was the couple's bloody bedroom. Five nights had passed since the stabbing and it appeared that Susan had been working frantically ever since then to clean up the room. Despite her efforts, the place still looked exactly like a murder scene. There was still blood just about everywhere detectives looked. There were so many individual drops, stains, and spatters, it was going to be a major pain to document and catalog all of it and then get samples of each significant drop that could be tested for evidentiary purposes.

The third major point of interest was the small enclosed back yard where the wooden bed frame had been disassembled and piled in pieces next to an obviously blood-saturated mattress.

It didn't take any major investigative skills to figure out that Jeffrey Wright had probably been stabbed in the bedroom and that, at some point during or immediately after the stabbing, his body—either just barely alive or just barely dead—had gushed blood onto the couple's bed.

The main elements of the crime appeared to have been concentrated at this one house on Berry Tree Drive. There was no sign of blood in the couple's vehicles out in the driveway, no indication that there were any other places the detectives should be looking for additional clues.

The puzzle now confronting the investigation was to figure out what the body and the other pieces of evidence could tell them about the circumstances under which this person had been stabbed and the sequence of events that led up to the stabbing.

It was once believed that the eyes of murder victims were permanently fixed with the image of the person who killed them—like a final snapshot. The notion, which made for macabre tales in more superstitious times, has since been discredited, but today the modern science of forensic investigation does let the bodies of the dead tell secrets about their killers.

It may seem odd, but it is the murder victims' very humanity—their "humanness"—that helps investigators when the victims can no longer speak for themselves.

If someone finds a ten-dollar bill lying in a vacant lot, there's almost no way to know how long it has been there or whether it was lost or stolen or put there intentionally. However, with a human body, every single detail is in some sense significant. The simple fact that people are alive imparts a fundamental logic to every moment of their existence. They have to breathe, they have to eat, and they have to sleep. Beyond that, there are places they belong and things they have to do that fill in their lives. But, for all their seeming variety, no living person can be placed in a drawer or sit abandoned in some field like a junked car for days or weeks on end.

Living people can do a tremendous amount of things, but there's an equally large number of things they can't do or aren't likely to do, and it's those intrinsic limits to what is realistically possible that let detectives build up a time-line for the victim's last hours that in turn can shape the outlines of the murder investigation. Piecing together the logic of the victim and his circumstances tells investigators volumes about what could or couldn't have happened to him in the minutes, hours, and days preceding his death. The trick is figuring out what the dead person is saying—because he's definitely saying something.

It took detectives hours to carefully unearth Jeff's body. It was stiff with rigor mortis and showing some early signs of decomposition, but as the investigators worked with trowels and paintbrushes to remove the dirt, they immediately noticed a couple of significant features.

The first and most obvious thing was that the body was naked, and it had suffered a spectacular number of stab wounds—dozens upon dozens of them. They ranged across his body, but the ones to his head had completely obliterated his facial features. From the quick inspection detectives were able to make as Jeff was being lifted from the household grave and placed into a body bag, it was also clear that this blizzard of injuries had been almost entirely inflicted upon the front of his body.

The second feature of interest was a set of ligatures of some sort tied around both of the wrists and around the left ankle. A closer look made it clear the

ligatures had ends hanging loose that had been cut,
but still remained firmly tied to Jeff. That suggested
Jeff had been tied to something at some point during
or after the killing.

It was becoming clearer to investigators what must
have taken place in the bedroom.

After Jeff was zipped into the body bag, put on a
gurney, and taken out to the waiting hearse for a trip
to the morgue, the investigators began putting all of the
loose dirt from the gravesite through a sieve. By the
time they were done, they were confident that they had
gotten everything that'd ever gone into this particular
hole back out of it.

Investigators that Saturday evening didn't have an
opportunity to interview Susan—in fact they had no
clue where she was—but they did have access to the
sworn statements that she'd given to the Family Violence Unit just three days before at Precinct 4 when
she reported that Jeff had been abusing her.

Susan had reported seeing Jeff Monday night and
then again on Tuesday morning. The last time he'd
been at work and talked to anyone else that investigators knew about was Monday, so they were comfortable guessing that Jeff had been buried for only a few
days—but out there on the patio there was just no
quick way to tell exactly which day he had died.

Detectives considered that Jeff may have heard
through the grapevine that the police were looking to
arrest him. Susan had already mentioned one violent
return home on Tuesday, so Jeff might have come back
after that and attacked her in another of his rages.

As the weekend progressed, detectives were able
to interview Susan Wyche. She told them the little bit

of information she knew about Jeff 's death that she'd gleaned from her conversation with Susan on Saturday morning. Wyche said that her daughter had confessed to killing Jeff and putting him in a hole, but said it had happened because Jeff was about to kill her.

Police were prepared to hear Susan's side of the story—and send the case on to a grand jury that might write the whole tragedy off as self-defense and decline to indict her.

What the officers really needed in order to determine what they were dealing with—a clear-cut case of justified self-defense, or perhaps something more sinister—was an autopsy.

7

As the Harris County Medical Examiner, Dr. Dwayne Wolf had seen his share of murder victims, but even to a hard-bitten professional like him, the corpse of Jeffrey Wright was a gruesome sight to behold.

It fell to Wolf to figure out how many times Jeff had been stabbed, and to determine what each of those wounds could tell him about the homicide.

Dr. Wolf ended up spending Sunday examining Jeff literally inch by inch. He drew a map of the stab wounds, bruises, and other injuries he was able to identify, measuring the width and depth of each one of them looking for clues. There were so many wounds on Jeff's chest, neck, and head that many of them overlapped. That made it difficult for Dr. Wolf to distinguish in the most severely damaged areas whether he was looking at an individual stab wound or a layered pattern of several stabs. By the time the night was over, Dr. Wolf would be able to identify 193 separate stabs—but at the same time, because of the overlapping action of the attacker, he was confident the real total was somewhere over 200.

The most interesting thing about the pattern of the wounds was that, with only one or two exceptions, they had all landed on the front of him. This was puzzling because almost anyone who is being attacked with a knife, especially with repeated thrusts coming straight at him, will instinctively put his arms out front and back away from his attacker in an effort to defend his most vulnerable spots—the head, throat, and upper torso. That is why so many stabbing victims have "defensive wounds" on their hands and forearms—it's a classic indication of an attempt to fend off a knife assault in the most obvious and logical manner. But while Jeff had plenty of stab injuries on his arms, and a few on his hands, the single largest concentration of wounds on his body—at least forty-six distinct strikes—was on his chest. Specifically they were in his upper left chest.

Police were already leaning heavily towards Susan as their suspect. Even if Dr. Wolf and the investigators hadn't had another single clue to work with in the Wright case, the mere fact that Susan had been able to plunge a knife into Jeff's chest nearly fifty times, when he was nine inches taller than she was and a hundred pounds heavier, without his being able to stop her, would have raised a red flag for prosecutors.

But those stabs to the chest weren't the only injuries Jeff had suffered. Dr. Wolf also counted twenty-three in his neck, twenty-two to the abdomen, another seven plunges of the knife into Jeff's groin area, and a series of small slicing cuts to Jeff's penis. Again, these were all areas that any conscious person would be expected to defend even more vigorously than their extremities. The rest of the wounds, over a hundred in all, ranged up and down Jeff's arms and legs and into his face. Jeff had been stabbed straight through one of his eyeballs, and the knife had been stuck again and again into his head. An x-ray revealed that the missing point of the hunting knife was lodged in the top of Jeff's skull, where it had broken off during the furious assault.

Dr. Wolf probed all of the wounds looking for the most significant: the one that had actually killed Jeff Wright—perhaps a slice through the heart, a lancing of the jugular—but in the end, came up empty. Despite the astronomical amount of times Jeff had been stabbed, not one of the wounds was actually fatal in and of itself. Dr. Wolf concluded that it was the loss of so much blood and not the trauma, grievous as it was, that had actually caused Jeff Wright to die. The average healthy adult male has about a gallon-and-a-half of blood in his body. Jeff, at 220 pounds, would have had a bit more, but the circulatory system can't cope with much blood loss before the drop in blood pressure causes shock to set in and begins a rapidly spiraling chain reaction of major organ failures leading to death.

There was nothing to indicate that Jeff had tried to staunch any of the bleeding or retreat from his attacker. It's a simple medical fact that living people bleed when cut and bruise when bludgeoned, but dead people don't. Thus, it was possible for Dr. Wolf to tell from his careful examination that somewhere on that Monday evening Jeff had died in the midst of the attack. This was obvious to the trained expert because, while many of the stab wounds had been inflicted on a living victim, many of them had not.

Somewhere along the line Jeff had plainly bled to death and his attacker, apparently oblivious to that fact, had continued stabbing him.

Rolling Jeff's body over, Dr. Wolf took a careful look at his back. Here the story was much different. There was a single significant stab wound midway down Jeff's right shoulder blade, but the fury that had been vented on the front of Jeff's body seemed never to have arrived back here, even though it was clear from the analysis that whoever stabbed him had kept right on going even after he'd died.

In addition to the single distinct stab wound, there were also some minor surface injuries on Jeff's back—small abrasions really—but the interesting thing about the series of scrape marks was that they appeared to have occurred post-mortem. The scrapes backed up the detectives' conclusion that the body had been moved at some point from the bedroom out to the patio.

Despite all the details that had to be checked and double-checked, the main issue confronting Dr. Wolf that Sunday was the question of how Jeffrey Wright had been overtaken and killed. How could a healthy 220-pound man, a man who'd been to a boxing lesson that very evening, have been overpowered, possibly, by a 120-pound woman, to the point where she was able to stab him a couple of hundred times while only sustaining superficial injuries herself?

The element of surprise, or perhaps just dumb luck, made it theoretically possible that Susan could have inflicted an incapacitating injury during the initial seconds of a stabbing. But nowhere in the vast collection of wounds on Jeff's body did Dr. Wolf find any such single incapacitating hit. Instead, it looked like Jeff had suffered horribly, including the blow through his eye, but had been unable to muster a competent defense. The reason seemed obvious: the ligatures that were around Jeff's wrists and his left foot.

Lying on his back and firmly tied down to a wooden bed frame, even a 220-pound man would be a sitting duck for anybody with a weapon. Given that kind of tactical advantage, Susan could have taken her time and killed Jeff with just about any item in the house. So how could Jeff have wound up in such a compromising position? Again the answer seemed obvious. Jeff was naked and it looked like he had been tied up with a couple of neckties and a bathrobe sash. It didn't take too vivid an imagination to picture his pretty wife getting him to submit to a little kinky bondage followed by hot sex.

There was one other small but crucial piece of evidence that Dr. Wolf found that led investigators to conclude that Jeff and Susan were involved in some sort of bedroom game in the minutes before the stabbing commenced. It was a trail of red candle wax which had been drizzled down Jeff's naked inner thigh towards his groin. It had dried hard against his dead skin.

Even though it would take until Monday for the dental records to arrive and allow for a positive identification of the body, what had happened now seemed all too clear: Jeff Wright had let his guard down in the sanctuary of his own home, in the privacy of his own bedroom, with the candlelight flickering, in the presence of a woman he'd been married to for four years. He'd allowed himself to be rendered utterly defenseless by a woman who—whatever the ups and downs of their overall relationship—he clearly trusted was about to treat him very well indeed.

Dr. Wolf had looked over the body to see what Jeff Wright could reveal about his own murder and the answer seemed to be that Jeff had been seduced into the bedroom, lulled into an unbreakable trap, and then methodically slaughtered.

The authorities came away from the autopsy table determined to put Susan Wright behind bars for the rest of her life.

8

On Monday, January 20, 2003, Jeff's murder hit the Houston papers.

Unlike a lot of crime stories where the first news accounts are sketchy, major elements of the Wright case were made public right off the bat, because the investigation had actually been under way for a couple of days before reporters got wind of it.

The investigators hadn't talked to Susan yet, so they weren't ready to officially call her their suspect, but they had immediately fanned out and spoken to nearly three dozen of the Wrights' family members, neighbors, and friends. Since the police knew they had their killer identified, and it appeared that for all practical purposes she had already confessed to the crime, albeit by hiring an attorney, the Harris County officials were comfortable releasing a lot more information to the press than they would have in a normal investigation— where there would have been a greater effort to withhold key details that only the killer would know.

The Wrights learned about their son's death in the most impersonal of ways. They had been checking the *Houston Chronicle*'s website on Monday to see if there had been anything about their missing son when they came across a breaking news item saying he was dead and that Susan had admitted to killing him. "We were shocked and stunned to first find out about it online rather than being contacted," Ron Wright told the Associated Press. "You just can't imagine what that feels like."

Newspapers and television stations in Houston reported that Jeff Wright had been stabbed 193 times by his wife and that her lawyer was saying she'd done it because she feared Jeff would kill her and harm his children.

Police were quickly getting their conclusions out to reporters. Lieutenant Daniel Billingsley, the homicide chief of the Harris County Sheriff's Department, explained that the victim had been completely buried at one point, but the Wrights' dog had partially unearthed the body.

Billingsley also told reporters that it appeared Susan, or someone anyway, had made efforts to clear away the crime scene at the house. "There are certainly indications to us that there's been evidence of an attempt to conceal or destroy evidence," Billingsley said.

"We have a lot of work left to do," he added. "While her attorneys say she's admitted to this, she has not admitted it to us, and until we finish investigating, I'm not willing to say she's a suspect."

Officials also told the press about Susan's remarkable visit to the constable's office a few days earlier, where she reported that Jeff was missing and that she was the victim of abuse. "She had told a neighbor that if they saw him on Wednesday, the fifteenth, 'If you see my husband, call police,' " Billingsley said.

Harris County Precinct 4 Constable Ron Hickman told reporters, "She alleged the typical family violence kinds of things: evidence of contact wounds and bruises."

Defense attorney Neal Davis knew what issues the prosecutors would look at as they considered filing charges, and launched a full-court press with Houston's print and television media.

Davis sat down with reporters and explained that Susan was as much the victim here as Jeffrey, that she had acted purely in self-defense, because she thought her crazed husband was on the brink of killing her and her two children, and that she was suffering from severe psychological issues and undergoing treatment at a psychiatric hospital even as they spoke. "She acted to protect herself and her family. She was a battered wife," Davis told the *Houston Chronicle* in one interview.

"There are family members, friends, and physicians who have personally witnessed the bruising and scarring from the abuse. The next step for us is to continue cooperating with the police," Davis told interviewers. However, he said it would be at least another week before he would allow detectives to interview Susan.

Davis detailed his fateful trip out to Susan's house on Saturday afternoon and explained how he'd had her sister come and get the children before he'd checked her into the psychiatric facility.

Davis also noted that there was a marijuana possession conviction on Jeffrey Wright's record, and described him as a heavy drug user who'd recently punched his young son twice in the face.

"Basically she really only had two choices: She could either kill her husband or he would kill her and their children," Davis told the Associated Press. "He beat her the whole time. This is not some manufactured defense after the fact. Her family saw the bruises and the scarring. Friends saw it and the doctors have seen it. He told her if she said anything about the beatings, he would kill her and the children. A while back she went into hiding [the signs of abuse]. She went into a life of covering up."

Commenting on reports that Susan had buried Jeff in the back yard, Davis said, "She just wanted to get him out of the house."

Over and over Davis repeated that Susan had been battered. In a television interview Davis stressed that Susan had not reported any of the abuse previously because Jeffrey had threatened the lives of her and the children if she ever told anyone. "I've tried to emphasize that family, friends, and at least one doctor have witnessed the scars and bruising that she received at the deceased's hands over time," Davis said that Tuesday. "I'm not surprised at all that some may not know of this abuse."

When they stepped up to reporters' microphones, officials were careful to note that Susan was not going to be accused of anything until police had a chance to sit down and question her about the night Jeff died. Investigators briefly raised the possibility that they might be looking for additional suspects; however, behind the scenes those same officials were convinced they were now looking at a grand pageant play being acted out by Susan Wright in an effort to save her skin in the wake of a truly savage killing.

Behind the scenes, the police had access to the stack of interviews that had been conducted with Susan's friends and relatives, and were increasingly convinced that Jeff had been killed on the night of January 13. That put Susan's visit to Precinct 4 on January 15 in a completely different light. Standing there talking to Constable Hall, Susan had to know that Jeffrey had been buried under her patio. As far as the cops were concerned, it looked like a clear attempt at a cover-up.

Each day detectives sent an updated report of all their evidence to the district attorney's office. Since this case was not shaping up to be a "whodunit," the only real question was whether or not authorities were looking at a justifiable claim of self-defense. Once the Harris County DA's Office thought they had received a complete picture of Jeff's killing and the context surrounding it, they would have to make a decision on whether or not to have a grand jury indict Susan for murder.

Davis' characterization of the Wrights' marriage shocked even their close friends. "I've never seen Jeff show anything but love to those kids and to his wife, and no one knew," said the Wrights' neighbor, David Flick, one of Jeff's best friends, in an interview with News 2 Houston. "That's what's so mysterious about the whole thing."

If friends were shocked by the image of Jeff as a crazed drug abuser who was smacking around his young children and threatening to kill his wife, then Jeff's family across the state in Austin was just flat-out stunned by the accusations. "My son is being portrayed improperly," Ron Wright said. "She was not abused." Within hours Ron Wright was defending his son to anyone who would listen.

"He never abused her, that's just factual," Wright told a journalist. "The first time an abuse claim was filed was after she killed him. I could imagine she'd have some marks on her if someone were fighting for his life while he was getting stabbed numerous times."

The next day, Tuesday, investigators sat down with the Wright family in Austin and heard their opinions on their son and daughter-in-law's marriage.

The Wrights told police that, in hindsight, they thought Susan had killed their son on the night of January 13, probably just minutes before she had called them. The Wrights had been trying to follow the events of the past week from a distance, frantically calling relatives around the country for any word of Jeff. They had to figure out what they could from Austin and had tried to make sense of the fact that when they called Jeff's cell phone, it was still at his house—and so were his keys and his truck.

Back on Berry Tree Drive in Houston, the Wrights' house had been locked up tight and barricaded with crime-scene tape. But even though the forensic investigators had wrapped up their searches and photographed and seized everything that looked to be related to the crime, they still hadn't been able to carry out one of the most important parts of their investigation.

Detectives urgently wanted to speak to Susan and hear what she had to say on the record about the death

of her husband. They knew from Davis' statements to
the press that Susan was in a psychiatric ward, presumably in the Houston area, but because of attorney–client
privilege, Davis was under no obligation to tell them
exactly where.

That didn't mean that the prosecutor's office
couldn't use every method at its disposal to turn up
the heat on Susan. With over 200 stab wounds on Jeffrey, they didn't think they were looking at a real self-
defense case anyway. Prosecutor Kelly Siegler quickly
issued an ultimatum. Either Susan showed up by noon
on Friday to tell her side of the story, or she was going to be charged with murder.

It was already pretty clear to Davis what the mood
was over at the prosecutor's office, so, faced with the
near-inevitability of a murder charge anyway, this
wasn't a major threat. Davis fully expected Susan's
case to go directly to a grand jury at some point. It
was also true that Susan couldn't expect to hide in a
hospital indefinitely. Regardless of her mental state
she was going to end up in custody sooner or later,
and Davis knew that it would be better to do it on his
terms than the state's.

On Wednesday Kelly Siegler told reporters that she
had made a decision to go ahead and charge Susan.
Siegler had the preliminary autopsy report and the interviews in which Susan Wyche had said that her
daughter had confessed that she'd killed Jeff. It was
enough to proceed with, and on Thursday, Siegler
filed formal murder charges against Susan.

"Susan Wright is wanted for the murder of her
husband and is not in custody," Sergeant Tommy
Kiser told the *Houston Chronicle*. "We have no idea

where she's at. [Davis] is telling us he has her checked into some psychiatric hospital somewhere. We asked if he could have her brought up to talk, and he declined."

Talking to the *Chronicle* himself a short time later, Davis responded, "She's been in a terrible mental state. She's just way too fragile psychologically to talk to [the detectives] and undergo hours of interrogation."

Since the authorities still didn't know exactly where Susan had been stashed, it gave her a chance to have a visit with her children and her sister Cindy. It also allowed her to consult with Davis as her inevitable arrest approached.

Davis announced mid-week that on Friday morning Susan would show up with him at the Harris County Courthouse and turn herself in.

9

On Friday, January 24, 2003, Susan surrendered herself to authorities at the Harris County Courthouse in downtown Houston. At the request of police, Davis had arranged for her to turn herself in ahead of her arraignment, which had been scheduled for the following Monday.

Accompanied by Davis and her mother, Susan Wyche, Susan came into the courthouse at 9 A.M. and was formally charged with murder and ordered held without bond until her arraignment. The murder charge carried a potential sentence ranging from five years' probation to life in prison.

Davis took the unusual step of asking to have Susan released on bond prior to her arraignment, noting, "As you can see, she's very, very fragile. She's been in psychiatric care."

Kelly Siegler didn't budge. Known for her sharply tailored suits and her even sharper tongue, Siegler had been to the house at Berry Tree Drive to see Jeff's body. She was not the least bit inclined to cut Susan any slack. "No one else gets that treatment," she said.

"She's a murder defendant. She shouldn't be treated any differently than anybody else. She can wait until her case is on the docket on Monday."

Siegler told the court that Jeff had been stabbed 193 times in a murderous attack, not an act of self-defense. "When it happened, he was tied down to his bed by his wrist and ankles."

In most cases where murder is charged, the defendant's attorney does not begin by admitting to the court that the defendant actually killed the victim. Davis acknowledged that his client had done the deed, but quickly added, "Susan Wright was having serious psychiatric problems that were the result of four years of mental and physical torture by her husband. She's been beaten for four years and verbally abused, her son was struck at least twice by the deceased—photographs support that."

Prosecutors said that initially they had been prepared to believe Susan Wright was in fact a victim, but her story just didn't square with the evidence they'd found, especially once the full autopsy report came back to them on Thursday, the day before this hearing.

"The medical examiner's office has determined that he suffered from one hundred ninety-three stab wounds and incising wounds upon his body," Sergeant Tommy Kiser said. Kiser repeated the investigators' theory that Jeff had been tied down to the bed when he was murdered, in part because so many of the stab wounds were to Jeff's face, eyes, neck, and groin.

Siegler argued that this case was flat-out murder. "Self-defense means you're in immediate fear for your life or your children's lives. What can a man strapped down to a bed do to you when you're holding at least one knife? How is that self-defense?"

As a huge jurisdiction that had already seen plenty of murder cases, Harris County had a set legal procedure and bail bond formula in place for dealing with murder defendants.

With her arrest officially concluded, Susan Wright was facing charges that carried the very real possibility that she could spend the rest of her life in jail. Whatever the outcome of her eventual trial, this weekend would be the first time in her life she would be behind bars.

Susan may finally have been in custody but, on the insistence of Davis, she was still not going to face a police interrogation until he was ready for her to do so. "The possibility of us having her speak to police at some point is not off the table," he told the Associated Press. "It's just right now, she's in no condition to withstand questioning, much less give a statement. We'll show there's a logical and reasonable explanation for the events surrounding his death."

While Susan sat in jail that Saturday in Houston, across the state in Austin, the Wrights were having to bury Jeffrey.

The funeral service at the Anderson Mill Baptist Church was packed with relatives and friends from the neighborhood where he grew up. It concentrated on the good things that people remembered, from Jeff's birth in Kenosha, Wisconsin, some thirty-four years earlier, to his life in Texas in both Austin and Houston, and finally to his love for his young children, whom he had delighted in showing off on visits back to his home town.

A short time later Jeff was laid to rest with a graveside service at St. John's Cemetery in nearby Georgetown.

In a statement, Ron Wright said, "Saturday our family buried our beloved son. The church was full. Our hearts are overwhelmed with the support of all the people who knew and loved Jeff. Now we must start the battle to clear his name and see that justice is done."

Ron Wright also vowed to fight for custody of his two young grandchildren. "Our family would appreciate the continued prayers for the well-being and safety of our grandchildren. Children's Protective Services has been contacted, as we now know what their mother is capable of doing. The children are precious and endearing to our family."

On Monday, January 27, 2003, Susan was brought back to the courthouse for a bail bond hearing. Her mother and sister watched from the benches.

The main purpose of the morning hearing was just to determine whether Susan was a flight risk and whether releasing her would pose a danger to the community. Since there was little doubt that Susan had killed Jeffrey for reasons that were probably unique to her circumstances as his wife, it was clear to the court that if she was released, she wasn't likely to go out and hurt somebody else. That left open the question of whether she would flee; it didn't seem like the mother of two was going to skip town, so prosecutors asked for the standard bail amount that gets set in similar cases in Harris County—$30,000 cash.

In making their arguments, the prosecutors showed a bit more of the evidence they had gathered against

Susan: affidavits that quoted various investigators about specific details of the case. In that paperwork the press got its first hint of the frantic activity that Susan had engaged in in the days just after Jeffrey died, when she'd tried to tidy up the bloody mess.

Siegler noted that Detective Mark Reynolds had searched the Wrights' bedroom and found it "contained paint, paint rollers, and freshly painted areas. The carpet had been cut out of the bedroom, some areas of the room had been bleached, and bleach containers were still present in the trash can." Several areas of the bedroom walls had been freshly painted and sections of the bedroom carpet had been cut away; other sections had been bleached. Despite those efforts, Detective Reynolds noted that he and the other investigators found blood spattered on the walls, ceiling, bedroom furniture, and in several other areas throughout the house, as well as on the headboard, mattress, box spring, and bed frame they found in the back yard.

Reynolds also noted that the ten bags of topsoil they found by the patio matched the type that had covered Jeff's body.

Siegler also filed a partial transcript of the police department's interview with Susan Wyche in which Wyche said that Susan had admitted to her that she had killed Jeffrey in their bedroom. " 'Mamma, I wasn't me. I snapped. I was up there and I saw somebody do it, but it wasn't me,' " Wyche told police, quoting her daughter. During her interview, Wyche also told them that Susan had said she'd killed Jeffrey with a knife on the night of January 13 and "He was in the hole he dug."

Davis tried to get Susan's bond set at $10,000, but Siegler argued strongly that any such move would represent preferential treatment, and something of a tacit nod towards innocence, for a woman whom Siegler was convinced was a cold-blooded murderer.

Siegler mocked the notion that the standard bond amount was excessive, pointing out that Susan had spent the better part of a week in an expensive mental health care facility. Siegler's other exhibit was Davis himself. She argued that anyone able to hire an attorney from the prestigious Houston law firm of DeGuerin Dickson & Hennessy was obviously somebody who could afford to post the normal bond. "Why give her a special bond? If you have a seventeen-year-old first offender charged with possession of one gram of cocaine and he has to make a normal bond, why shouldn't she?" Siegler asked.

In the end Judge Jim Wallace agreed with Siegler and set Susan's bond at $30,000. Wallace also ordered Susan to give a saliva sample for DNA testing before she even left the courtroom. A sheriff's deputy had Susan step aside after the hearing and he took a swab from the inside of her cheek, then sealed it in a plastic evidence bag.

Susan was returned to jail briefly following the hearing, but late in the afternoon on Monday, with the Wyches' help, she posted bail and left with her relatives.

Talking to reporters after the hearing, Siegler attacked what already clearly was going to be the defense's main argument: that, although it was Jeffrey who died, it was actually Susan who was the victim in the case.

Siegler deflected the questions about whether or not Jeff had been abusive, pointing out that in Texas, as in so many states, the question of whether or not Susan had committed murder or been legitimately defending herself would boil down to her actions the evening that Jeff had died, not his actions during the preceding four years.

"Do you think that rises to the level of self-defense, when you have someone tied down to a bed, each wrist and foot tied up?" Siegler asked. "Is that where you're in immediate fear for your life or your children's lives? Where I come from there's another answer for that, and that's divorce.

"A jury one day will decide whether or not she's a battered wife."

Asked about the prosecution's assertion that any history of abuse was really beside the point, Davis said, "We believe we can show she was defending herself and her children, and the prosecution's theories are purely speculative at this point.

"She was being abused, physically and emotionally, and so was the little boy—the four-year-old boy," Davis said. "My main goal is just to get her out of custody so that we can see if she needs more treatment, but I would suspect that she probably does."

10

Trials always seem to take a long time to get started, mainly because of the volume of behind-the-scenes legal work—the pre-trial motions, depositions of witnesses, examination of experts—all of which goes on largely out of public view.

But while the Wright case was awaiting its day in court, there were a couple of points which were not lost on trial watchers. The first was that the trial was going to take place in Harris County—home office of the death penalty in the United States. Because she had no prior criminal history and had only killed one person, as well as several other technical factors, Susan wasn't on trial for her life but she would still be faced off against the prosecutorial staff from one of the harshest law-and-order jurisdictions in the Western world. To top it off, Prosecutor Kelly Siegler was chief of the Major Offenders Division, and a legend of a prosecutor in what was already a legendary prosecutor's office.

Just the fact that a female prosecutor was assigned to the case made life difficult for Susan's defense team. Susan would've normally had a slight psychological edge going into the case simply because she was a woman. Consider for a moment if the tables had been turned on the evening of January 13 and it had been Jeff who stabbed Susan 193 times. If he had then gone to trial claiming he did it in self-defense because of domestic abuse, he would have had the proverbial snowball's chance in Hell of succeeding. But as a woman trapped in a bad relationship with a controlling husband who dabbled in drugs, Susan was potentially a much more sympathetic figure, who could conceivably sway a jury to her side.

That argument would be much easier to advance if she were up against a male assistant district attorney who would have to be careful not to look like he was further beating up on a poor abused widow and mother. But pairing Susan off against another woman, a woman who wasn't buying her story, would not invite the kind of protective backlash among the jurors that an aggressive male prosecutor might have generated.

The other thing that made the choice of Siegler inherently difficult for the defense was just that she was Kelly Siegler.

Siegler had a reputation not just for winning, but for winning spectacularly. Difficult, unusual, headline-grabbing cases were made even more memorable by the tactics Siegler employed.

Siegler had joined the Harris County District Attorney's Office in 1987 after having come out of the middle of nowhere—a small town called Blessing, two hours southwest of Houston—where she had grown up. There, she'd watched her father, the local barber, who doubled as the town's justice of the peace, call together jury trials when necessary and hold them in the local feed store.

Kelly Jalufka was the little girl who had loved to read and who went on to be the star student in her high school class of just forty-four students. She spent three years at the University of Texas, where her dormmates quickly nicknamed her "the Hick" because of her small-town background. She had originally set out to be a smooth corporate lawyer, but soon discovered she couldn't take the tedium and switched career paths to the rough-and-tumble action of the criminal courts downtown.

Kelly married Dr. Sam Siegler, after she met him on a hunting trip to Blessing when he was a medical student. By the time the Wright case began, Kelly Siegler had just turned 40 and she and her husband had two daughters.

When she came to court the brunette Siegler was always an elegant figure in tailored suits, but it was as much a mistake to dwell on her appearance as to dwell on her rural Texas accent and homespun demeanor. None of those things hurt Siegler in the least, but what made her a devastating opponent was that she took the time to really prepare for her cases. Catching Siegler off-guard was not something defense attorneys got to dream about, let alone count on, when they were up against her razor-sharp prosecutions.

Houston's media loved to tell Siegler's story as she moved her way from major case to major case. In December 1999 the *Houston Chronicle* ran a profile of her under the headline "One shrewd cracker-barrel lawyer."

Chronicle reporter Steve Brewer began the piece by talking about how Siegler's father Billy Jalufka used to give haircuts in his bare feet in his barber shop and don a clip-on tie when he needed to officiate as the town's judge.

"I practice every argument and time it out like I'm in that barbershop," Siegler was quoted as saying in the piece. "I figure if I can talk to a jury like I'm explaining it to Daddy and his buddies, then I'm doing okay."

As Brewer put it in the *Chronicle*, "Siegler's self-described 'good-old boy' approach, flair for the dramatic and disdain for what she calls 'lawyer talk' has earned her the respect of defense lawyers and coworkers alike. Many of them say she is the best trial lawyer in the district attorney's office."

Siegler didn't just edge out courtroom victories—she steamrolled the opposition. She shredded defense witnesses, humiliated defense attorneys, and creamed liars right in front of rapt jurors who sided with Siegler's simple, earnest, down-home logic of justice time and time again.

Siegler loved being a prosecutor because she liked the moral high ground and the opportunity to hammer the bad guys. In an age of irony, cynicism, tolerance for the aberrant, and a basic reluctance to judge others, Siegler allowed jurors to see cases where the defendants were arguing among shades of gray in stark black-and-white terms of justice.

With Kelly Siegler on her case, Susan wasn't just facing eventual prosecution—she was facing a hurricane.

Siegler's story would have been unique pretty much anywhere, but the fact that she'd come from

Blessing and now was at the Harris County Prosecutor's Office, in the thick of its hair-raisingly intense trial action, was flat-out amazing.

Harris County sends more people to death row than any other county in Texas—in fact, more than any other county in America. If Houston were a state instead of a city, it would rank number three in the nation for death penalty convictions, behind only the rest of Texas and Virginia.

Harris County plays for all the marbles when it brings a capital case and, depending on how you look at it, Kelly Siegler is either one of Harris County's most effective prosecutors—or one of its most zealous.

By the time the stage was set for Susan Wright's trial in early 2004, Siegler's success rate was staggering. She had won convictions in 95 percent of the cases she had prosecuted and in all but one of the seventeen capital cases she had argued, the jurors had come back asking for the death penalty. The one who got away had had his case end in a mistrial when a pregnant juror suddenly went into labor, hardly any fault of Siegler's.

Siegler had an innate ability to present the gory details to juries in a manner that helped walk them through difficult decisions. Having her as an opponent didn't augur well for anyone's defense, and Harris County had put her on Susan Wright's case from day one.

Siegler's talent didn't go unnoticed outside of Texas either. She made *The National Law Journal*'s list of the top fifty female attorneys in the country in December 2001. In 2002, the *Journal* went one better and listed her as one of the top forty lawyers in the country, period—dropping the separate male–female listings.

If her colleagues had any reservation about Kelly Siegler (aside from the alarming prospect of being assigned to a case in which she was going to be the opponent), it was the lingering concern that she might actually be *too* good at prosecuting people in front of juries.

The legal system can be a deadly dull choked with protracted hours of endless dry paperwork. Tedious nitpicky little details dog everything from utility right-of-way easements in real estate contracts to evidence collection and chain-of-custody issues in murder cases. Every fall television season seems to feature a new slate of dramas that make police stations, lawyers' offices, and courthouses look like exciting venues in which a non-stop circus of human emotion pours out in fascinating waves of activity. Television shows rarely feature cops spending endless hours looping through empty parking lots during 3 A.M. patrols or prosecutors typing out rebuttals to sixty-page defense motions to suppress confessions. So the fact that Kelly Siegler managed to turn real-life cases into riveting and epic battles was something to be appreciated in its own right.

But for all their genuine admiration of Siegler's presentation skills, defense attorneys in Harris County also wondered what was going to happen if someday a defendant who really should have gotten the benefit of the doubt—a defendant for whom reasonable people could have reasonable doubts—found himself up against the irresistible force of her self-assured viewpoint that potentially complex and tangled phenomena could be reduced to straightforward narratives and judgments.

That concern cropped up in a television interview with famed Texas defense attorney Richard "Racehorse" Haynes, whom *Time* magazine had described as one of the top six trial lawyers in the country.

Speaking with CBS reporter Richard Schlesinger on an episode of *48 Hours,* Haynes had high praise for Siegler, saying that she "whipped me like a rented mule!" during their face-off in court in a death penalty case that Siegler handily won.

"She is absolutely excellent. First of all, she's intelligent as hell. She's good-looking, that don't hurt," Haynes noted wryly. But a moment later he voiced the same concern that several people had expressed over the years about Siegler's stunning ability to grab the attention of a jury and shred any witness in the box. "She's so good at what she does, it bothers me that her skills are going to overpower the facts and somebody will be doing time for a crime they didn't commit."

Despite all the checks and balances, no one has ever figured out how to invent a perfect justice system, and Hollywood has made an industry out of showing how mysteries and murders can end with unexpected twists that clear the person whom everyone suspected. Long before movies and television dramatized how the least likely person in each situation could actually be the killer, the Founding Fathers of the United States developed a system that was supposed to address those concerns. Only people who are guilty beyond a reasonable doubt are supposed to be convicted. If a jury thinks there is an excellent chance the defendant did exactly what they are accused of, but has just one nagging reasonable doubt about an aspect of their guilt, then they are supposed to walk that person right back out the front door of the courthouse on the presumption that they are innocent. The problem with the theory is that no one, especially the vocal majority who are *not* on any jury at the moment, wants to let a guilty person get away with something horrible. The public doesn't want crooks, thieves, and killers getting sent back into their midst on a "technicality." Since one person's reasonable doubt can quickly be labeled a technicality by irate observers, there is in real life a great deal of pressure on juries to make sure that they don't let the bad guys get away.

11

Houston was still buzzing about Susan Wright, even a year later when her trial started on February 23, 2004.

For reasons that even Texans have trouble explaining, the Lone Star State seems to produce if not more than its fair share of crazed female killers, then at least more memorable ones than anywhere else.

There was beauty queen Clara Harris, who ran over her husband with her Mercedes; Wanda Ann Holloway, the "Texas Cheerleader Mom," who tried to have the mother of her daughter's high school cheerleading rival assassinated; Andrea Yates, who drowned her five young children in a bathtub and blamed Satan; and Yolanda Saldivar, the president of singer Selena's fan club, who turned on the blossoming star and gunned her down.

It was against this backdrop of high-profile lethal women that Susan Wright burst into the headlines. But unlike a lot of the other notorious female defendants, Susan had been allowed to post bail. She was even allowed to visit her children, who were supposed to be staying with her sister Cindy, but when the judge learned that Susan had quietly moved the children back in with her, temporary custody was awarded to Jeff's parents in Austin. Still, Susan was allowed to travel to Austin on the weekends to continue having supervised visits with Bradley and Kaily.

Jeff Wright's death had been just the second homicide committed in Houston in 2003 out of what would eventually be a total of 278 murders that year. Houston's homicide rate had been steadily dropping since 1981, when it had soared to over 700 killed—a spike that was attributed to the city's boom-town atmosphere at the time, and to the arrival of Detroit serial killer Coral Watts, who police are now sure killed at least a dozen Houston women that year and maybe dozens more.

In any event, it takes something unique for a murder to capture the imagination of the imaginative city of Houston, but the Wright case had managed to do so. It was often featured in headlines and on the teases for TV newscasts as "the buried husband case" and Susan was always mentioned as the former stripper who had lost it. But, despite all the lurid interest, the substance of the trial was expected to be fairly straightforward.

Everybody knew Susan had done it. She was even prepared to admit that she had done it. There was no doubt Susan was the person who had stabbed Jeffrey Wright at least 193 times on the night of January 13, 2003, thus causing his death. The real questions confronting the jury in the 263rd District Courtroom were going to be: Exactly what did Susan Wright do that night and why did she really do it?

Within hours of the discovery of Jeff's body, Davis had begun getting Susan's side of the story out to the press. He'd made no secret of the fact that Susan was going to present a defense that was kind of a one-two punch to explain her actions. First she was going to argue that she had killed Jeff in self-defense and then she was going to argue that what appeared to be an effort to cover up his death was really more of a period of temporary insanity brought on by both the trauma of the killing and lingering psychiatric problems from four years of having been a battered wife.

In the last decades of the twentieth century, the public got its head firmly wrapped around the concepts of domestic violence and spousal abuse. Along with countless other offenses that once used to be "just the way things were"—like drunk driving and making fun of ethnic minorities—domestic violence went from being nobody's business to being something that was talked about on public service announcements and at city council meetings.

At first volunteer groups and then entire communities put together shelters for battered women. Police departments changed policies and procedures to ensure that when they encountered people who hit family members, those people ended up getting prosecuted whether or not the victim wanted charges pressed.

Today it's difficult to watch an old episode of *The Honeymooners* without noting that in our times, if Ralph Kramden had ever actually hit Alice hard enough to send her "to the moon," he would have spent at least that night in jail, followed in all likelihood by months of sitting on a metal folding chair taking court-ordered "cognitive self change" courses in some community center, alongside all of the neighborhood's other domestic abusers.

It was against that backdrop of support for the abused, at least within the legal system, that Susan Wright went to court in 2004.

Even in Texas, which seems to take kind of a perverse pride in executing people right and left even while other states are wracked by questions of moral and evidentiary uncertainty, there's an inherent sympathy for a woman who is being cowed and battered in her own home, especially one who is trying to do the right thing to protect young and vulnerable children.

To prevail at her trial Susan Wright would have to convince at least one juror that it was reasonable to believe she could have been in the midst of defending herself from an attack when she snapped after four years of abuse and simply went off the deep end when it came to stabbing her abuser. Such an argument would not be the same thing as an actual insanity defense, which would have required her to argue that she was out of it to the point that she didn't know it was wrong to stab Jeff in the first place.

Insanity defenses were really a thing of the past in Harris County since the 2002 trial of Andrea Yates, the 37-year-old Houston mother who had drowned her five children in a bathtub and then called 911 saying, cryptically, "It's time." Even though an appeals court would grant Yates a new trial in 2005, the fact was that a Harris County jury had initially found that Yates wasn't suffering from insanity when she committed the murders, so that pretty much ruled out any future insanity pleas by anybody in Houston who couldn't be shown to be barking mad upon their arrival in the courtroom.

Self-defense was a different story. In Texas, which has a long and distinguished history as a frontier state where armed cowboys and lone rangers had to mete out justice on the spot, lawyers were able to stand on the steps of the courthouse and say with a straight face that there's a legal theory in Houston that "some people just deserve killing."

From a purely legal standpoint, it really didn't matter whether Susan went on and stabbed Jeffrey 193 times or 1,930 times in a fit of pure undiluted psychotic raging orgiastic bloodlust and revenge, *provided* that the very first time she stabbed him that evening was in fact a legitimate act of self-defense.

There was one thing about Susan's defense that the jury wasn't supposed to consider—but it was plainly there when they thought about it. It was that in the thirteen months since Jeff had been killed, the Harris County District Attorney's Office had also had plenty of opportunity to think over Susan's version of events and consider the question of whether or not her actions amounted to justifiable self-defense.

If the assistant DAs had looked over their evidence and felt Susan was telling the truth about striking back in a legitimate act of self-defense at a husband who was seconds from killing her or harming the kids, then either the prosecutors or the grand jury could have decided to drop the charges against her. Other cases in Texas where wives had killed husbands had been reviewed and established as self-defense, and the woman in question had been walked right out

the front door of the police station without a courtroom showdown. But Kelly Siegler had considered
Susan's story. After reviewing it, she not only thought
Susan was lying about what she had done to Jeff and
the reasons why, Siegler also thought she could prove
it to a jury beyond a reasonable doubt.

Siegler was so confident that Susan was toast, she
didn't bother to offer Davis a plea bargain to consider. This case was going to trial and Siegler was
prepared to fight it right down to the wire for the sake
of Jeff and his family.

12

Late on the afternoon of Monday, February 23, 2004, just over a year after Jeffrey had been killed, a panel of twelve jurors and two alternates was seated in the warm burnished-wood surroundings of Judge Jim Wallace's courtroom. What was expected to be a two-week trial would determine who was the real victim in the Wright household that fateful night—Jeff or Susan.

The question of media exposure weighed heavily on the mind of Davis and the other members of the defense team as they had quizzed the potential jurors.

Much time had also been spent discussing the definition and legality of self-defense with the potential jurors, and seeing if any of them had problems in their own past dealing with divorce, domestic violence, or the use of deadly force.

The seven men and five women who made the final cut had all answered "No" on their jury questionnaires when asked "Would your verdict be affected by gruesome photographs?" and said "No" again when asked "Would you be affected by knowing this trial will be broadcast on national television?"

The 263rd District Court was indeed going to be in the spotlight for the duration of Susan's trial, and everyone seemed to be conscious of the camera. Susan had strode into the courtroom first thing and taken a seat behind the defense table. Her family and the Wrights had quickly sorted themselves into uncomfortable proximity on the front benches of the packed room.

During a break in the proceedings, Davis spoke briefly about Susan with the press. "This incident has been very traumatic on her," Davis told reporters, "and the fact that she was charged with murder has been very difficult. We are looking forward to vindicating her in this trial."

Davis also said that he would show the jury photographs of scars and bruises Susan had suffered at Jeff's hands to back up statements from friends and relatives that Susan had been abused. "As we've said from day one, Susan has been the victim of an extremely physically, emotionally traumatic relationship, and we intend to show the jury that she acted in self-defense."

It was one of the last interviews Davis would give for a couple of weeks, because on Monday afternoon, before everyone left the courtroom, Judge Wallace brought up the "unusually emotional nature" of the case and ordered everyone involved—attorneys, court staff, and law enforcement—not to speak to the press until after the trial was finished.

Opening arguments on Tuesday morning started off with a bang.

Together the prosecution and the defense had sent out subpoenas to over seventy potential witnesses, but regardless of how many of those they actually chose to call to the stand, it was already clear that the two marquee players in this case were going to be Susan Wright and Kelly Siegler.

The burden of proof in the case fell to the prosecution, and by long-standing custom, that made Siegler both the first and the last person to present her side to the jury.

Siegler knew from the start that the biggest obstacle facing her was that Susan Wright was a young, pretty blonde woman with two little children. Susan simply didn't appear to be the kind of person the state would haul into court to face a trial for murder.

"Ladies and gentlemen, the anger, the lies beneath that beautiful blonde façade is unfathomable. She looks like someone you would never think could be a murder defendant," Siegler began, standing only a few feet away from Susan. Looking especially striking in a beige suit piped with black trim, Siegler continued, "This case is not about self-defense. This case is about selfishness."

Siegler noted that Jeff had taken out a $200,000 life insurance policy on himself, and that Susan would've rather gotten that check than any considerably less valuable divorce settlement.

Siegler described the Wrights' four-year marriage to the jury as troubled, failing, and destined to end. But, she said, Susan Wright had had religious qualms about getting a divorce. So Susan began to scheme about another way to get a new life without Jeffrey. Siegler said Susan had thought up a scheme to lure Jeff to his death with a promise of sex, seducing him, tying him up to the bed frame and then letting him have it with a knife so she could walk away with the $200,000 policy. Why Susan would have had *less* religious reservations about first-degree murder and insurance fraud than divorce, Siegler didn't say.

"She committed murder in the most brutal, horrific, unbelievable way you've ever seen," Siegler told the jury panel who sat riveted in front of her. "She took that knife and stabbed him everywhere in the front of his body. She took that knife and she stabbed him in the eyeball. She took that knife and she stabbed him in the mouth. She took that knife and stabbed him in the ear. She took that knife and nicked at his penis. What should have been a love nest, what should have been a night of lovemaking, turned into a torture chamber. Blood was everywhere."

Turning from the killing to the weird week that had followed, Siegler told the jurors about the missing persons report, the trips to Target to get paint, the stories Susan told Jeff's co-workers and police about Jeff leaving and returning and then leaving again. To Siegler these were clearly the efforts of a frantic murderer in a race against time to construct an alibi. "Posttraumatic stress syndrome? How about cover-your-tail syndrome?" Siegler asked.

When it was his turn to put forward an opening argument, Davis told the jurors that Susan had indeed killed Jeffrey—right after he had come home "hyped up" on cocaine, hit his 4-year-old son, and then raped and beaten her.

"For years before this incident, Jeffrey Wright had kicked, pushed, and punched Susan Wright," Davis began. "He told Susan that if Susan ever left him, he would kill her or he would kidnap those kids."

Davis argued that the killing frenzy she unleashed on the evening of January 13 was completely uncharacteristic of Susan. "She's a peaceful person," he said. "We're gonna bring you witnesses to talk about how Susan is a nurturer."

It was only as a last resort to protect herself and her two young children, Davis argued, that, following several days of escalating violence, Susan had finally gotten the courage to fight back. Her marriage had long since turned on her, but when Susan looked up from the bed moments after having been forced to have sex with Jeff, she saw him standing over her with a knife, Davis continued. "She wrestled the knife from Jeff and out of the maternal instinct to protect her kids, she stabbed him," Davis explained. "At that point Susan had a total psychic break with reality. She sees herself from above, looking down stabbing Jeff. That's a total break. She goes and she gets a necktie and ties his hands to the bed and she continues stabbing him. Out of sheer terror she stabbed him over and over again."

In Davis' view, the hours and days after she killed Jeff proved how out of it Susan had become. The fact that she had frantically tried to clean up the house so Jeff wouldn't be mad about the mess, that she had told police and friends that he was just angry and absent instead of dead and buried, that she had stayed up for almost five days without sleep clutching a knife in case Jeff returned to attack her again—all these bizarre actions were the result of post-traumatic stress syndrome from the horrific stabbing, from the rape which had preceded it, and from the years of emotional and physical abuse that she'd endured up to that fateful night, Davis argued.

Minutes later Davis himself would become part of the evidence as one of the first witnesses to testify in the trial, Assistant District Attorney Terese Buess, took the stand. Buess recalled the night of January 18, 2003, when Davis had come in to her office building out of the blue and reported that he knew where police could find a dead body. Buess remembered the stunned reaction of the staff, and Davis adding that he couldn't give any other details because of attorney–client privilege. "He was very shaken; his hands were shaking very badly," Buess testified.

13

On Wednesday prosecutors rolled out what would be, in Siegler's hands, their most dramatic piece of evidence.

State's Exhibit Number 56 was a genuine showstopper—the actual deathbed where Jeffrey Wright had met his end at the point of Susan's knife.

Detectives carried in the large wooden pieces of the king-sized bed frame and began rebuilding it on the open section of floor in front of the defense table, just inches from Susan. She gazed at it in horror, raising her hand to her chin and beginning to shake noticeably as it was put together.

Short of dropping Jeff's perforated corpse right into the middle of the courtroom, the still-bloodstained bed was about as graphic as it was possible to get. Audience members and even jurors gasped as deputies set the mattress atop the wood frame and it became clear that the large angry-looking stains still covering both were actually Jeff's blood—lots and lots of it.

Sitting just a few feet away, Ron Wright began wiping tears out of his eyes.

The bright, almost Day-Glo pink bedspread that had been recovered from the back yard was laid down on top of the mattress and once again jurors could clearly see at least one large bloodstain prominently near the center of it.

That the bed was mesmerizing just about everyone in the courtroom was not lost on Davis. Susan couldn't even bring herself to look at it, and people were glancing from it and back to her again as the real horror of the display in front of them began to sink in.

Davis quickly rose to object. "It's overly theatrical and I think it's overly prejudicial to the jury," he started, but he was quickly overruled. Whatever histrionics Davis detected in placing the bed on public exhibit were about to be totally eclipsed by Siegler, who was preparing for an actual theatrical performance.

Siegler, wearing a black suit jacket and matching black pants, turned to the jury and pointed out that she herself was approximately the same height, weight, and build as 5' 5", 120-pound Susan Wright, seated a few feet away across the defense table. At the same time, Siegler pointed out that her colleague, Assistant District Attorney Paul Doyle, was about a hundred pounds heavier and approximately a foot taller, just like Jeffrey Wright.

With that, Siegler asked Detective Mark Reynolds to tie Doyle to the bed using the same kinds of neckties and knots that had been found attached to Jeffrey Wright's wrists.

"Based upon your observations of the photos, and the neckties themselves, show the jury the way the left wrist was tied," Siegler began as Judge Wallace invited Davis to leave the defense table and stand by the bed, where he could keep a closer eye on the demonstration.

Without hesitation, Doyle, wearing a white dress shirt and tie, lay right down on the mattress, atop Jeffrey's year-old bloodstains. Reynolds expertly looped a tie around the wrist.

"Similar to that, tied around his wrist," Reynolds said as he finished. "And then?" Siegler asked, indicating Reynolds should lift the tie to show the jury.

"What I have left is from here down," Reynolds said, showing the loose length of the tie that would have remained dangling out the other side of the knot.

Siegler asked Reynolds to go ahead and attach the loose end to the bed in whatever manner he thought would have been "similar" to the way that Susan must have done it.

Reynolds began to tie it around the bedpost above Doyle's head. When the body had been found, only the knotted part of the necktie that was attached to Jeffrey was still intact. As to precisely where and how it would have been tied to the bedpost, Doyle explained, he was "speculating."

The word immediately struck Davis, who stood next to Reynolds watching intently. "I think, Judge, I'm going to object. Even the detective said this is speculation, I mean . . ." Davis began.

Judge Wallace considered the presentation and replied, "Well, the jury should understand that as far as the exact location as to where, and if, this ligature was tied to the bed, that's not being presented as the exact spot—is that correct?"

"Yes, sir, it is," Siegler responded.

"Really?" a surprised Wallace responded.

Siegler explained that the detectives had looked over the bed and the position of the bloodstains and determined that the corner posts were the most likely point at which the ligatures had been attached to the structure of the bed. With that, Wallace let the demonstration go forward.

"Okay, do you have both of his wrists tied tightly?" Siegler continued.

"Yes, ma'am," Reynolds answered.

"Paul, try to lift your hands up," Siegler urged the prone Doyle.

It only took Doyle a second to indicate that his full range of motion was only an inch or two.

"Okay," Siegler nodded. "Now, same thing for his ankles."

Davis stepped forward again. "Same objection on the ankles too, Your Honor. It's all speculation. The manner of the knot itself also needs speculation."

"I understand that it's for demonstrative purposes," Judge Wallace said, overruling the objection once again.

Siegler commented, "Okay, now you're tying the robe sash a little differently," as Reynolds looped the cloth through the slats at the end of the bed. "Explain to the jury what you are doing, based on what you saw in the photos."

"It's just a single knot tied in the middle of the sash around the ankle, and there's another knot tied in this fashion and it's broken in this area here," Reynolds explained as he worked to duplicate the knot police had photographed.

"Okay," Siegler noted, continuing, "And hold it up for the jury to see where you saw the sash broken."

Reynolds did so, gesturing to where the item had been severed. "Between whatever it was tied to and here," he noted, fixing the tie to the bedpost and then picking up another piece of sash to tie Doyle's right ankle, his final free extremity, to the remaining corner of the bed.

Once again, Davis spoke up. "I'm going to object to this, Your Honor, because I believe the testimony is that there was one sash recovered. We've got two here."

"There was a sash recovered, Judge," Siegler countered. "But based on his opinion as a police officer, because there was another sash recovered out in the yard after the dog had been after the body, that's the reason we believe both feet were tied up."

Davis wasn't budging. "I object to that. There's just no basis for that. One sash was recovered and this is just theatrics. Object."

Judge Wallace had the attorneys approach the bench and after a short discussion out of earshot of the jury, the lawyers returned to where Doyle had been lying patiently.

"If I understand the court's ruling, for now, Judge, then we'll leave this foot untied," Siegler resumed, gesturing to Reynolds. "Will you take this one off?" she prompted, pointing to Doyle's ankle.

Davis had technically won the argument over Doyle's right leg, but the jury had certainly seen what Siegler was getting at, and she was still free to argue that all four of Jeff's limbs had been tied down during the actual stabbing.

"For purposes of this demonstration, how about if you stand at that corner right there, right by Mr. Davis?" Siegler said. "Detective Reynolds, based on the photos and the injuries you saw on the head of Jeffrey Wright, which were more significant, those on the right side of his face or on the left?"

"Most of the injuries were targeted to the left side of his face," Reynolds said.

Reynolds had just given Siegler the opening line to what was going to become the single most memorable half hour of Susan Wright's trial.

"Okay, and, Judge, if I could?" Siegler looked at Judge Wallace, who knew what was coming next.

"You may," Wallace nodded.

Playing the part of Susan on the night of the stabbing, Siegler stepped out of her shoes and climbed right up on the bed, putting her knees on either side of Doyle's waist, straddling his supine form. Taking the Schrade USA "Old Timer" hunting knife with a three-inch blade in her right hand, Siegler resumed her line of questioning with Reynolds.

"All right, so if the defendant were to get up on top of Jeffrey Wright, something like this, and straddle him, and she's right-handed, then how do you think she held the knife? Put it in my hand." Reynolds arranged the oddly curved knife so Siegler and the jury could see the classic downward plunging grip associated with every scary stabbing movie since *Psycho*.

The jurors, like everyone else in the courtroom, were riveted by the pair's demonstration. It was hard to imagine a more effective way that the prosecution theory could have been put forward. The whole scene was having a clear emotional impact on Susan, who began to snivel and cringe as she sat rigidly behind the defense table turning away from what was being staged right in front of her.

It was something that no defense attorney likes to see in the middle of a court case: a clear, compelling demonstration why the evidence points to his client having done things exactly the way the prosecution was alleging. Davis again tried to defuse the drama. "This is just all speculation. Objection. I mean, 'How do you think she held the knife?'" Davis asked incredulously.

Judge Wallace prompted Siegler to explain it. "If we can go with questions a little more to the witness as to how he comes to conclusions as to how the knife was held."

"Yes, sir," Siegler replied, turning her attention back to the detective. "Based on the injuries that you saw and the direction of the cuts, tell the jury why it was that you believe the knife was held that way in my hand."

"The locations of the injuries themselves are slicing, and they are top to bottom lengthwise," Reynolds began.

"In other words, vertical instead of horizontal?"

"Yes, I believe it was vertical."

"And that would be consistent with the knife going in this way." Siegler demonstrated another downward stab.

"Correct."

"Vertical, not this way, horizontal," Siegler reiterated, moving the blade from side to side.

"Correct," Reynolds noted.

"And is it a more natural fit in your hand to do it this way, as opposed to this way?" Siegler asked, stabbing again at the assistant DA.

"Yes, ma'am," Reynolds agreed.

"Okay, so if I'm on top of Paul and I'm holding it this way in my right hand and I attack at the head area first, which side of his face are most of the injuries going to be on?" Siegler wondered.

"On the left side."

"On his left side, which is right here. Is that right?"

"That's correct," Reynolds concurred.

"Okay, and most of the injuries were where?" Siegler prompted.

"Straight into the left side of the head."

Her main point made, Siegler swung a leg over and stood up once again beside the bed as Doyle continued to lay spread-eagle, tied to the frame.

"Do you recall the photograph of the injuries in the area of his penis?" Siegler asked.

"Yes," Reynolds replied.

"Okay. If I wanted to do stab movements to his penis, did you see anything consistent with a stab to the penis?"

"Not to the penis itself, no," Reynolds said.

"Because you saw what?" Siegler asked.

"It was nicked. There was a superficial cut. More of a slicing."

"Superficial slicings like this. Okay . . ." Siegler demonstrated a sawing motion with the hunting knife in the air above Doyle's groin.

"Right," Reynolds concurred.

Judge Wallace interjected. "I'm not sure that the jury can see your . . ."

"I'm sorry, Judge," Siegler acknowledged, turning so the jury could see her moves. "But more a superficial movement to the penis area, not a stab . . ."

"Not a penetrating stab," Reynolds agreed.

"Okay, how about to the rest of the body? Down there to the thighs, to the knees, to the legs, any injuries on those parts of the body?" Siegler asked.

"There were some injuries to the knees and the lower legs, but very few compared to the concentration above," Reynolds noted.

"Okay," Siegler continued. "Let's talk about, for just a minute, is there any way that the wounds could've happened down here to this part of his body if I were still straddling him like I was a minute ago?"

"I don't believe that would be possible." Reynolds shook his head.

"Okay, so it would be more consistent with my being where—to inflict the wounds to the leg?"

"On the side of the bed," Reynolds said.

"Not on the bed? But like I'm standing right now?" Siegler queried.

Davis spoke up. "I object to this as being speculation as well, Your Honor. I mean, there are any number of different ways he could have gotten those wounds on his legs in terms of position."

Siegler pressed onward. "I could ask it this way: Were there some wounds down here to the leg?"

"Yes," Reynolds said.

"And up in this area to the leg?"

"Yes."

"And is this side of the leg the side that's closest to me? The left side of his body?" Siegler probed.

"Yes, from where you are standing, yes," Reynolds agreed.

"Okay now, in the chest, where were most of the wounds concentrated on the body of Jeffrey Wright?"

"In the chest, in the neck, and the chin," Reynolds said.

"So we're talking about basically from above his belt to well below his chin?" Siegler noted.

"Yes."

"And could you tell where they were more concentrated in the chest area itself?" Siegler pressed.

"There was a great number of wounds, both penetrating and just incised," Reynolds said.

"Okay, now, again holding the knife the way you said to a little while ago, to describe the face, were all these injuries in the chest area consistent with the knife being held in this direction?" Siegler asked.

"No."

"Okay, what's the difference? What else did you see?" Siegler asked.

"You see wounds where the knife blade is what you would call horizontal. If we call this vertical, more horizontal," Reynolds said, indicating with his hands that some of the wounds had run from side to side across Jeff's torso.

"More this way." Siegler reiterated Reynolds' gesture. "So there were some wounds where the knife blade goes into the body at this direction?"

"Correct."

"Consistent with someone perhaps standing beside the body inflicting the wounds that way?" Siegler asked.

"Correct," Reynolds agreed.

Siegler and Reynolds had concluded their demonstration of the actual stabbing. It had only taken about twenty minutes to present, but when the newspapers and television began showing the images of Siegler sitting on top of Doyle stabbing at him with a knife on the very bed where Jeff had been killed, those few minutes quickly became the iconic image of the Wright trial that would remain in the public's mind.

Those snapshot visuals were so dramatic that they tended to obscure one of the more interesting points that Siegler had made during the course of her demonstration—that the stab wounds that covered the front of the body had come from two different directions. This suggested Susan had paused the attack at some point, changed her position relative to the bed, and then gone on and stabbed Jeff some more.

Although the jury would not get to hear much more about it for another week, the fact that there were some horizontal wounds in addition to the numerous vertical stabs could be interpreted as adding credence to Susan's version of the stabbing. By sitting on Doyle, Siegler had shown how awkward it would have been for Susan to have inflicted horizontal cuts across the chest and any of the injuries to Jeff's groin, legs, and feet from atop his lap.

Reynolds' answers to Siegler's questions had pointed out that, for at least some portion of the attack, Susan was most likely *not* straddling Jeff in the manner Siegler had demonstrated. Davis had already touched on this area during his opening arguments. Susan had admitted to killing Jeff in the bedroom. She'd admitted stabbing him around 200 times with the knife. But Davis had said that at some point after the initial struggle, Susan had overcome Jeff, stopped the attack, then tied him to the bed and resumed stabbing him. So far, nothing in Siegler's demonstration had directly contradicted Susan's version of the event.

Siegler began to ask Detective Reynolds to untie Paul Doyle from the bed, but Davis leaned in and whispered a request to her. Siegler nodded and turned to Judge Wallace. "Mr. Davis asked me, so we don't have to retie Paul up later, if we could demonstrate better his ability to move his hands, so let's do that." Wallace concurred. "First of all, Paul," said Siegler, "move your left hand up as far and as high as you can."

Doyle lifted his left arm maybe three whole inches above the surface of the bed and immediately his motion was stopped solidly by the necktie.

"That's as high as you can go?" Siegler asked.

Doyle nodded.

"Okay, move this foot up as high and hard as you can."

Again Doyle's motion was barely perceptible.

"Okay, and if I'm sitting on top of you and I'm holding a knife, move your hands up like you are trying to get me," Siegler urged.

Jurors leaned forward to watch Doyle's response. Fingers curled and wrists raised only slightly, it was obvious that anyone restrained like that couldn't begin to struggle, let alone fend off an attacker.

"That's all you can move?" Siegler confirmed. When Doyle nodded, she turned back to Davis. "Is that good for you?"

"That's fine," Davis replied.

Watching the demonstration progress, Judge Wallace realized that it would be awkward to keep having to tie and untie Paul Doyle to the bed during the day and he decided to change the usual order of questioning a bit.

"Now, Mr. Davis, do you want to do any cross while we have the person on the bed in this position?" Wallace inquired.

"Yes, Your Honor, please," Davis replied.

As bad as things had looked as the demonstration progressed, Davis knew there was a fundamental point which held true for a lot of murder cases that was also holding true for this one. Namely, that whatever particular sequence of actions the prosecution might have convinced themselves had to have happened, it was still an undisputed fact that Susan had been the only other person present when the killing took place.

No matter how clever a demonstration Siegler and the other investigators put forward, Susan could only be convicted if the jury believed that the scenario acted out before them matched the evidence from the crime scene and the autopsy. In that regard Davis thought he was holding at least one ace—the single prominent stab wound to Jeff's back below his right shoulder, and a series of jabs into the backs of Jeff's legs.

Walking past Doyle on the bloody bed, which was still sitting in the middle of the courtroom, Davis tried to raise doubts about the prosecution's version of the stabbing.

Davis wondered how Jeffrey Wright could have been stabbed in the back, even just once, if he'd been tied down to the bed in the manner the prosecution had demonstrated. Turning to Reynolds, Davis started in. "This may be a little uncomfortable, but here's what I want to ask you, Detective: You said that you looked at the body at the scene, correct?"

"Yes," Reynolds acknowledged.

"Also, Miss Siegler talked about a bunch of injuries in this area. There also happens to be a wound over, if I can point it out to the jury, back here near the shoulder blade, correct, on the back?" Davis noted.

"I think it was in this area right here," Reynolds said, indicating a spot on the back near the underarm area.

"Okay, why don't you point it out to the jury where it was?" Davis prompted.

"I think, without looking at the pictures, but I think it was in this area right here. Some type of stab wound," Reynolds reiterated.

"Okay, was there also some in the leg area, on the back of the leg?" Davis asked.

"Yes."

"Okay, why don't you show me on my leg where those were?"

"I would have to look at the photos to tell you exactly where they were. There was a number. There's a very few, most of them were to the front or side, but as I recall, there is . . ."

Judge Wallace interrupted Reynolds' presentation for a moment: "I don't know that the jury can see that. Step over in front of the demonstration. Now, if you'll demonstrate again what you were saying . . ."

Davis put his foot forward helpfully. "If I put my leg up here, why don't you point out, on my leg, where

Police found the mattress, with prominent bloodstains, in the back yard behind the Berry Tree Drive house. (*Harris County Sheriff's Office*)

Police found Jeff's pickup truck right in the driveway, despite reports that he'd stormed off and left five days earlier. (*Harris County Sheriff's Office*)

The Wrights' typical living room with their kids' toys, as police found it during their search. (*Harris County Sheriff's Office*)

The shallow grave where Susan buried Jeff. He'd dug it earlier to install a fountain. (*Harris County Sheriff's Office*)

Bloodstains on the mattress. (*Harris County Sheriff's Office*)

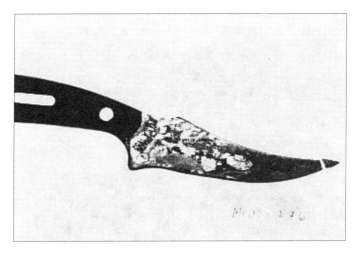

Detectives found the bloody knife on the patio, just a few feet from the body. The tip was recovered from Jeffrey's skull. (*Harris County Medical Examiner*)

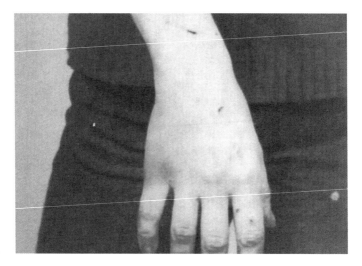

When Susan showed up at Precinct 4 saying she'd been the victim of abuse, she showed police scrape marks and bruises on her hands and legs. (*Harris County Sheriff's Office*)

Attorney Neal Davis said that from the day he met Susan he thought she had undergone a "complete psychic break from reality." (*TV pool*)

Prosecutor Kelly Siegler questioned every aspect of Susan's version of events. (*TV pool*)

Neal Davis holds up a set of nunchucks in court. He argued that Jeff used weapons to terrorize Susan at home. (*TV pool*)

Detective Mark Reynolds took the stand and explained why he thought Jeff had been tied up before the stabbing commenced. (*TV pool*)

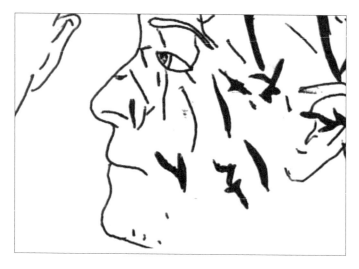

A medical examiner's chart shown to the jury mapped the dozens of stab wounds that Jeff suffered. (*Harris County Medical Examiner*)

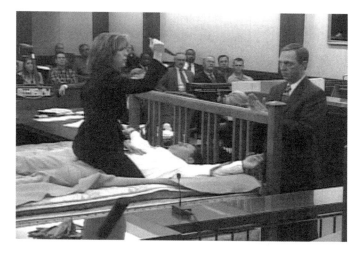

Siegler acted the part of Susan atop Paul Doyle as Detective Reynolds described how he thought the stabbing transpired. (*TV pool*)

ABOVE: The vivid picture Siegler painted as she acted out the murder was brought up repeatedly by Susan's defense team as they appealed her conviction. (*TV Pool*)

CENTER: The sight of the reenactment brought Susan to tears. (*TV pool*)

BELOW: Siegler demonstrated several angles from which she thought the knife blows had been delivered. (*TV pool*)

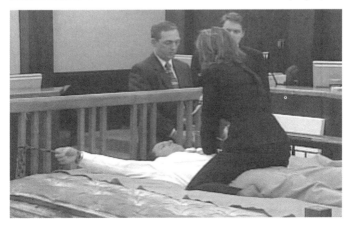

On the stand, Susan tearfully denied that she'd been angry enough to deliberately torture and then murder Jeff. (*TV pool*)

else there were some injuries on the deceased in this case?"

Leaning over, Reynolds began to indicate several spots on the trouser leg of Davis' suit. "As I recall, there was a couple of puncture wounds, stab wounds, to the backs of the leg."

"But it's on the back side of the leg, correct?" Davis stressed.

"Right," Reynolds agreed.

"Just to be clear," Davis continued, "I think I pointed to my left shoulder, and, I know you don't have your notes, but the stab wound on the back was actually on the right shoulder, do you recall that?"

"I'd have to look at the notes or the photos to specify that. I know there was a stab wound to the back. It was not the center of the back. It was towards the side," Reynolds said.

"Now, just to be clear, and of course, you're just speculating, but you suspect that all limbs were tied down, is that what you are saying?"

"Yes," Reynolds agreed.

"[Recalling] when Kelly was on top of him, you are talking about a knife wound that's back down under here, right?" Davis asked, sliding his hand down between Doyle's shoulder and the bed.

"On one side or the other, yes," Reynolds replied.

"Okay," Davis said with a hint of enthusiasm creeping into his voice. "You can't hit that part of the back from being on top of him, can you? You'd agree with me, wouldn't you?"

"No, I would not agree with you," Reynolds said.

"You're saying that if he's like this and tied up, and she's on top of him, somehow she can stab him towards

the center of his back below that blade?" Davis asked
skeptically.

"I believe it's possible to receive that injury,"
Reynolds said.

"How is it possible if he's tied up like that?" Davis
wondered.

"I'd think you'd be surprised at his mobility once
you've put that knife into his chest," Reynolds responded.

"Well, that's exactly my point," Davis shot back.
"That's exactly why I wanted him to show us where
he could move his hands. He didn't move them very
much, did he? And your testimony was that the ligatures were, quote . . . the ligatures were 'extremely
tight,' correct?"

"Yes," Reynolds agreed.

Pointing to the ties that still held Doyle to the bed
frame, Davis continued, "Does this, by the way, look
like six inches of tied 'extremely tight' to you? Is that
what you'd consider 'extremely tight' for a ligature?"

"I don't know how tight they were tied to the frame
of the bed. All I'm talking about was where they were
tied around the wrist," Reynolds answered.

"Oh," Davis responded, with a hint of sarcasm.
"Because again you are *speculating*."

He was finished, for now. Since he was technically
answering questions out of order anyway, because of
the unusual necessity of tying Doyle up in order to allow the demonstration, Davis yielded the floor back
to Siegler. She waited until Doyle had finally been
freed from Jeff's deathbed and then picked back up
with her interview of Detective Reynolds about his
portion of the investigation.

Asked if anything else unusual had been noted, Reynolds mentioned the red candle wax that had been drizzled near Jeff's penis. "It started in this area and went down between his scrotum and upper thigh," Reynolds pointed out.

Siegler asked if Reynolds had seen x-rays that had been made at the autopsy of Jeff's body, and he said that he had.

"What did you find, sir?" she wondered.

"There was a solid image in the top of the skull consistent with the tip of the knife point," Reynolds said.

At this point, nearly a half hour into the questioning of Reynolds, Susan was unable to keep her composure together any longer, and for the first time she began to sob openly in the courtroom.

With Doyle untied, Siegler began to set up another theatrical simulation. This time it was the rape scenario where Susan said she was able to wrest the knife away from Jeff. As Siegler got on the bed and Doyle prepared to climb on top of her, Davis launched another exasperated objection. "This is just complete speculation at this point," he argued. "If, after the jury receives evidence of what happened, then fine. But at this point this is all just speculation." Judge Wallace agreed and nixed the demo.

Following a break so the bed could be broken back down and removed, Siegler began her next area of inquiry for the jurors: the remarkable appearance by Susan two days after the killing, where she filed a missing persons report on Jeffrey and told police that he'd been abusing her for years.

Siegler pointed out that not only did Susan report Jeffrey missing, when in fact he was buried under the porch, but she also filled out the paperwork to apply for money from the Crime Victim's Compensation fund. Siegler hammered home the point about Susan seeking money in the wake of Jeff's death. This was the motive the state was trying to advance: that Susan had not killed out of fear, but out of sheer greed, that there was a $200,000 insurance payoff in her future if Jeff wound up dead.

When his turn came, Davis immediately switched the focus back on to the defense team's theory of the crime, that Susan was sufficiently terrorized by Jeff's abusive actions and constant little mind-control games that she had completely lost touch with reality by the night of January 13, 2003.

Davis asked Reynolds about an air rifle that Susan had said Jeffrey kept in their bedroom. Susan reported that Jeff had used it to threaten her on several occasions.

"If someone's killed and they're being shot by a pellet, of course, it would have to hit a certain sensitive area of the body. Or perhaps they're being beaten with a gun, it would be a deadly weapon in that case. Right? If the person died?" Davis asked.

"I believe so. Yes," the detective agreed.

In the wide world of firearms, air rifles can actually be bought as toys, but Davis wanted Reynolds to make the point that to Susan an air rifle, in the hands of a man bent on intimidating her at close quarters, could really have been an object of terror. It's rare, but people have certainly been killed over the years by a pellet shot from an air rifle and Davis wanted to show the jury ways that Jeff could have been creating overwhelming fear in his own home.

As Davis continued his questions, he read a sentence from the investigative report written by the detectives that noted that there were "defensive wounds" among the stabs to Jeffrey's hands. Davis suggested that the prosecutors themselves had just shown it would be unusual for defensive wounds to be found on Jeff's hands if his wrists really had been tightly tied down during the entire stabbing frenzy.

Davis also brought up the holes in the bedroom walls, where he said Jeffrey Wright had punched right through the drywall with his bare fists while in one of his rages. Davis implied that the investigators had skipped over those patched holes and instead concentrated on just the obvious bloody massacre scene in the bedroom and the wound-riddled corpse on the patio.

The next witness called to the stand would be brief and—when contrasted to the drama that had been played out just an hour or so beforehand atop the bed—would make a far less compelling story when it came to television and newspaper coverage the next day. But Katherine Welch, a DNA expert with the Harris County Medical Examiner's Office, would actually testify to the biggest near-miss of the entire case.

The whole point of putting Susan Wright on trial was really to determine one single question—had Susan gone after Jeff with the knife that night, or had Jeff gone after her?

Susan could frankly have been as loopy as she liked *after* the killing. She could have stabbed Jeff 193 times and then stabbed him another 293 times. She could have filed missing persons reports or claimed that she'd seen Jeff abducted by space aliens. None of that would have really mattered from a legal standpoint, *provided* that in the first few seconds of any violent encounter between wife and husband that evening, it was Susan who had been the real victim and not the aggressor.

From the moment she had come forward and contacted Neal Davis, Susan had admitted that she'd stabbed Jeff to death in the bed, and buried him in the patio, and cleaned up the bloody bedroom. None of those things in and of themselves proved that Susan had set out to murder Jeffrey in cold blood. The prosecution kept bringing them up because they certainly looked really bad individually and, when taken together, those things *suggested* Susan was acting in a manner inconsistent with that of an innocent victim. But, if Susan's accounts of the evening were to be believed, then all her subsequent bizarre actions were simply the behavior of a terrified person who had been driven over the edge of reason by persistent victimization.

Setting Susan Wright free would be as simple as believing what she said. If her story checked out, and Jeffrey's death happened the way she said it had, then she really would be the innocent victim of a horrific act of domestic violence and not a murdering schemer.

The core dilemma facing the jury was that, because there were no other witnesses to the killing, they would have to rely on each of the little clues left over from that evening of mayhem and then look at the circumstances before and after the killing to see if they could find any corroboration of Susan's version of events.

The one thing lacking from Susan's self-defense case was any shred of physical evidence—just one single clue—that Jeffrey had attacked her *before* she had gotten the upper hand and killed him with a flurry of knife stabs.

For all the drama of Kelly Siegler straddling Paul Doyle on the bed and showing just how many stabs it would take to get the count up over 200, what really mattered under the law was that very first blow of the knife. If Susan could show that Jeff attacked her first, she was free to go.

In years past it would have been impossible to prove or disprove Susan's story of a hand-to-hand struggle for possession of the knife. But thanks to the science of DNA analysis, in 2003 there was one small window of opportunity that could have provided an impartial look at that part of Susan's story and, if the results were positive, might have strongly suggested her innocence.

If there had been a struggle between Jeff and Susan for possession of the knife *before* she tied him up—if the bruises, cuts, and nicks on Susan's hands photographed at the precinct office two days later were in fact caused during the course of that struggle—then there was a good chance that minute traces of Susan's skin, even a few skin cells raked off her hands, would have ended up embedded in the material underneath Jeff's fingernails.

Such fingernail "scrapings" are nothing new to crime-scene investigators. It's a small trick of the forensic profession that has been used to great effect in dozens of trials around the country. It's a very effective way of proving that someone was involved in a hand-to-hand struggle with another specific person because the skin cells of that other person can be positively matched by DNA analysis. Usually fingernail scrapings are used to prove that someone was an attacker, not a defender, because the struggling victim gets some of the assailant's cells under the fingernails as he fights for his life. But in the Wright case there was an opportunity to show that Jeff was actually the aggressor, because if Jeff had Susan's skin underneath his nails, then he couldn't have had his wrists bound during some initial battle between them that evening.

Thus the material under Jeff's nails had the potential to be the pivotal piece of evidence for the entire case; however, Katherine Welch testified that the scrapings had been stored improperly after they were taken at the medical examiner's office. By the time the samples were unpacked to be sent on to the lab for DNA testing, it was discovered that mold had set in, and any chance of getting useful evidence from them had been destroyed.

The destruction of the scrapings didn't harm the prosecution case. Countless murder trials have been successfully prosecuted based on circumstantial evidence and the conduct and demeanor of defendants— even when the police haven't been able to find the body. But for Susan Wright, the loss of the scrapings was a devastating blow. They were the only noncircumstantial item in the entire case that could have potentially backed her up on the most significant and most disputed reason as to why she ended up killing Jeff that particular night.

There was nothing Susan and her defense team could do other than shake their heads and move on.

There was plenty of other evidence to consider, and lack of a particular piece, no matter how potentially critical, was not enough to get over the line into the land of reasonable doubt.

Moving on with what was already a busy day in the courtroom, the prosecution brought in a close friend of Jeff and asked him to discuss the state of the Wrights' marriage. He recalled it as a happy four years, characterized by the kind of peaceful domesticity that one would expect from two reasonable parents with two young children in a quiet neighborhood. He described Jeff as the kind of father who liked to play ball with his son and fire up the barbecue in the driveway.

During the cross-examination, Davis was more interested in what Jeff's friend could recall of Jeff's life prior to his marriage to Susan. The friend admitted that for years Jeff had been fond of strip clubs and cocaine. In fact, he acknowledged that Jeff had once been placed on probation for assaulting a stripper he'd briefly dated. Jeff had also pled guilty to a felony drug possession charge back in 1996 when he again got placed on probation.

14

On Thursday, with the bed reenactment still fresh in everyone's minds, the prosecution brought Harris County Senior Deputy Chief Medical Examiner, Dr. Dwayne Wolf, to the witness stand.

Dr. Wolf got out an anatomical chart, basically an outline of the front of a man, and over the course of the morning proceeded to map out every single stab wound that he was able to identify on Jeffrey Wright's punctured body.

It was a bewildering tally. Although the figure of 193 stab wounds had been a staple in the media coverage of the case, Dr. Wolf said he had actually been able to identify over 200 separate injuries on Jeff Wright's body. Out of those there were forty-six clear stab wounds to the chest—thirty of them right through Jeff's rib cage—twenty-three to the neck, twenty-two into the abdomen, seven in the groin, and one blow so deep into Jeff's head that the tip of the knife had broken off and was found still embedded within it.

The members of both Jeff and Susan's families, who had been present since Monday, began to excuse themselves as the morning's graphic testimony progressed. By the time Dr. Wolf was ready to start showing actual photos of Jeff's tortured body to the jury, both of the families were conspicuously absent from the courtroom.

The photos were indeed gruesome. As the jury studied each one, Susan again began to cry from behind the defense table. The sobbing eventually became so pronounced that Siegler asked her to try to contain herself.

There were so many stab wounds to discuss, accompanied by so many grisly photographs from the morgue that needed to be looked at, that for a while it seemed like an endless chore. But after several hours Siegler and Dr. Wolf had reached the end of the stack. As Siegler wound down what was by far the most disturbing portion of the prosecution's presentation, she had a final question.

"Did he die a painful death, Dr. Wolf?" Siegler wondered.

"None of these injuries would have caused instantaneous death," Wolf replied, "and there's no indication that he lost consciousness immediately from any of them. So, yes, I think so."

Amazingly, what had actually killed Jeff Wright that evening was not the numerous deep stab wounds that he had suffered. Instead, Jeff had simply bled to death during the course of the attack and the stabbing had continued on even after he had expired.

The only part of Susan's version of events that Dr. Wolf actually backed up was her statement that Jeff had been high on cocaine the evening of January 13, 2003. Dr. Wolf testified that the toxicology tests he'd run did come back indicating that Jeff had used coke in the hours right before he died, and he'd had enough in his bloodstream that he would still have been high at the time of the stabbing.

Siegler brought up a series of small scrapes that were found across Jeff's back. Asked how he thought those injuries had gotten there, Dr. Wolf said he thought they were post-mortem injuries that had occurred when Jeff's body was dragged by its feet down the hallway and out across the concrete patio.

This was actually an important piece of evidence that Siegler wanted the jury to fully appreciate, because if Jeff had been dragged, it would cast further doubt on Susan's initial explanation that she had tied the neckties to Jeff's wrists and ankles after the initial stabbing and then used them to secure his body to the metal dolly so she could move him out to the porch.

Once again, a bit of theater helped hammer home the point. Siegler got Dr. Wolf to lie on the floor, where she picked up his feet to demonstrate how Susan could have dragged the body and caused the scrape marks on Jeff's back and shoulders.

"So what you're saying is, he was grabbed around the knees and pulled like this and dragged like this?" Siegler asked as she tugged him a short distance across the carpeted floor of the courtroom.

Susan couldn't take this demonstration either, and looked away in tears as it continued. Eventually Judge Wallace politely asked the defense attorneys to keep Susan's emotional reactions to a minimum.

If Jeff had really been dragged out to his grave, rather than being tied to the dolly and then rolled out, it meant the neckties around the wrists and the bathrobe sashes around the ankles could have a much more sinister connotation. Siegler wanted to hear it from Dr. Wolf directly.

"He essentially had to be restrained when those wounds were inflicted," Dr. Wolf said. "That's my opinion, based on the pattern and distribution of the wounds."

Siegler also prompted Dr. Wolf to explain the noteworthy stab wound on Jeff's upper back that Davis had pointed to as evidence that Jeff couldn't have been restrained in the manner the prosecution was claiming.

She demonstrated an inward stabbing motion from what would have been the right side of Jeff's body. "[Say] you're trying to get loose and I have the knife. Could you stab somebody that way?"

"Sure," Dr. Wolf replied.

Dr. Wolf suggested the wound might have occurred as Jeffrey struggled to pull himself up or twist from side to side.

Siegler wondered what else Dr. Wolf could tell from examining the body that would shed any light on the events of that evening.

"Nothing about any of these wounds tells me anything about the state of mind of the assailant," Dr. Wolf replied.

"It's not every day where you see a body that has this amount of wounds to it, correct?" Siegler asked.

"Thankfully not," Dr. Wolf agreed.

During the cross-examination of the medical examiner, another member of Susan's defense team, attorney Todd Ward, asked Dr. Wolf about the wounds on Jeff's hands that at least one investigative report had described as "defensive."

How, Ward wondered, could Jeff have received more than a dozen wounds to his hands if they had been tied down and stretched above his head, at about the farthest point away from 5' 5" Susan?

Demonstrating on Dr. Wolf's arm, Ward asked, "Was it possible for his hand to reach over and touch the knife?"

"If his hands are tied here, and it's tied as tightly as you say, then he can't move," Dr. Wolf answered.

After Dr. Wolf finished testifying, the witness stand was turned over to Susan Wright's personal physician. He testified that he had seen Susan for ten years, including the four she was married to Jeff, and never once treated her for any injuries that could have been construed as domestic abuse. He also testified that on January 14, 2003, the day after Jeff's death, Susan had come into his office, where he checked out what he described as superficial cuts and bruising on Susan's right hand.

The next witness to take the stand was Harris County Deputy Constable Scott Hall.

Hall testified about the trip Susan made two days after the killing to the Precinct 4 offices to report that she had just been the victim of an assault and that it was all part of a long-running history of abuse at the hands of her husband. It was the first time that Susan had ever filed any sort of official complaint about Jeff, but it was a doozy.

That Susan's report story wasn't entirely truthful was not really what either side cared about. Instead, Hall was of interest to both sides because each had a diametrically opposed explanation as to why Susan hadn't told him the truth. To the prosecution, Susan's report was nothing more than a series of bald-faced lies designed to explain Jeff's sudden disappearance from the Earth on the night of January 13. The prosecution thought that the cover story would help to set Susan up as the victim when she eventually went to collect on Jeff's life insurance policy.

Hall testified that he'd asked Susan why, if she had actually put up with this kind of abuse for years, as she claimed, she hadn't gotten a divorce.

"She said it wasn't a Christian sort of thing to do, divorce," Hall said.

As Siegler was quick to point out, Susan's story then didn't quite square with Susan's story now—more than a year later.

"Did she mention anything to you, in this conversation that we talked about, about being raped?" Siegler asked.

"No, she never told me anything about being raped," Hall answered.

"How about her husband pulling a knife on her?"

"She never said anything about a knife," Hall said.

Siegler asked if Susan had indicated the marriage itself was in trouble.

"Yes. She said things were not working," Hall said.

On cross-examination, Davis asked Hall to describe, on a scale of 1 to 10, the level of fear Susan had displayed towards Jeff during their interview. "I believe ten would be accurate," Hall said.

Because Hall had examined and photographed Susan's hands and legs that day, Davis got to ask him whether he thought the nicks on her hands might be found on someone who was fending off a knife-wielding attacker.

"Do you agree with me that these might be defensive wounds from a knife?" Davis asked. "That these would be consistent with that?".

"They could be," Hall agreed.

Davis, who had already told the jury that Susan had experienced a "psychotic break" with reality in the days after the stabbing, wanted to know if, even in retrospect, Hall doubted her sincerity at all that day.

"It didn't seem at that time like Susan was trying to put on some charade?" Davis asked.

"Not to me at the time. No," Hall replied.

Next, the jury was shown a videotape made that day at Precinct 4, in which a Harris County Children's Protective Services investigator had interviewed Bradley. As the boy was 4 years old, the investigator was allowed to ask him a series of leading questions in a manner that would not normally be permitted in court if the person being interviewed were an adult.

As he crayoned away on a small table in the CPS playroom, Bradley said that he couldn't remember any instances of his father ever hitting his mother, but he did recall his father "punching me in the cheek," adding that it happened even though "I didn't do anything."

"He hit me one night, two nights, three nights, four nights," Bradley said.

15

With the investigators and the medical evidence out of the way, the focus shifted on Friday, to Jeff and Susan's friends and family.

The Wrights' neighbor, Jackie Davies, came to the stand to testify about the couple's relationship and her own close friendship with Susan.

"Did it seem like something out of *Leave It to Beaver*?" Davis asked.

"No," Jackie replied.

"Did it seem like something out of *Ozzie and Harriet*?" Davis continued.

"No," she replied again.

Davies remembered Susan telling her in the days after Jeff had been killed that there had been a fight because Jeffrey had hit Bradley.

"Jeffrey had gotten out of control and hit him," Davies testified. "She said it was one thing to hit her, but it was another thing to hit her kids."

At the time Susan was claiming that Jeff had left her and the children.

Asked to characterize what she'd seen of the relationship between Jeff and Susan over the years, Davies painted a picture of a disturbing relationship driven by Jeff, who came across as a domineering control freak.

"It was not a partnership. It was more of a father/subservient relationship," Davies said.

"Would you describe that as being a master–slave relationship?" Davis asked.

"Yes," she replied.

"And who was the master?" Davis asked.

"Jeff," she said.

"Who was the slave?"

"She was."

Davies recalled the week after Jeff disappeared as one of frantic activity, with Susan repeatedly calling friends and her husband's co-workers to see if they knew where he was. During the course of those calls Susan also told them that she and the kids had been abused by Jeff and that he'd walked out.

"She asked me if I had seen Jeff," Davies recalled, "and I said, 'No.'"

Neighbors assumed that at some point Jeff would probably reappear, just to collect his pickup truck and other belongings, if nothing else.

In a fascinating statement that helped back up Susan's self-defense claim, Davies continued that late that week, when she'd heard that police had been summoned to the Wright residence because someone had been killed, she didn't think the victim was Jeff. She just assumed Jeff had killed Susan.

The next to testify were Jeffrey Wright's parents.

His mother, Kay Wright, began by describing her youngest son as an easy-going, free-spirited sort.

"He was an adventurous person," she said. "He was a very friendly person. He never met a stranger. He just loved life."

Kay Wright described the disturbing phone call from Susan that had lasted over an hour on the night of January 13—a phone call that must have been made before Jeff's blood had even dried on the mattress where he died.

"I said, 'What's wrong?' and she said, 'Jeff hit Bradley in the face. I don't care if he hits me, but he's not going to hit Bradley,' " Kay testified.

The Wrights had actually spoken to Jeff on the phone earlier that same day and there had been no indication that he was in any kind of distress, or even upset. Certainly, after she hung up with Jeff, Kay Wright didn't have the impression that her son was on the brink of walking out the door and dumping Susan and the kids.

"He said, 'I love you, Mom,' and that was the last time I talked to Jeff," Kay recalled.

As Kay spoke about Jeff, Susan sat ramrod straight at the defense table and looked away from her mother-in-law.

Kay remembered that first distressed call from Susan clearly. She also remembered the frantic, miserable week that it touched off. Halfway across Texas in Austin, the Wrights spent days calling everyone they could think of in the Houston area who they thought might be able to find Jeff. If they could only get in touch with him, they felt, they would get some sense of what had prompted this bizarre outburst.

Kay and Ron took turns calling Susan back over the next few days, checking to see whether she had heard anything new. When they learned from Jeff's co-workers that he hadn't come to work and that his big GMC pickup was still parked in the driveway at Berry Tree Drive, they were even more worried. Susan told them that Jeff's keys and his cell phone were still in the house. It sounded like he had literally just walked out the door in the middle of the evening. But in Houston, geographically the largest, most spread-out urban municipality in the entire United States, you don't actually walk out. You drive.

The Wrights hadn't expected Jeff to cut out on his wife and children, but it made absolutely no sense to them that he would have done so and ditched his job, his friends, his family, and his vehicle at the same time.

To make matters even more confusing, Susan kept telling the Wrights that she had just seen Jeff. When they called mid-week they were told he had stormed back into the house and poured bleach all over his bedroom and then stormed back out. Susan kept putting on a performance intended to make them believe Jeff was still alive and that they had just missed him each time they rang. The baffled Wrights were trying to figure out where Jeff was going in between these crazed visits to his house because none of his friends in the Houston area had seen him since the night Susan first called them.

Kay described the horror and sadness one week to the day later, on the Monday after Jeff had been killed, when she learned that his body had actually been found two days before. It was only by chance when Jeff's older brother surfed onto the *Houston Chronicle*'s website that he came across a breaking news article that had just been posted. It was about the discovery of Jeff's body under the patio.

Kay turned right around and called Jeff and Susan's home number over in Houston, and Susan's mother, Susan Wyche, answered.

"I asked, 'Why did nobody tell us?' " Kay recalled.

"Why did you ask those questions?" Siegler asked.

"Because my son had called me and told me that he had seen it on the Internet," Kay replied. "He said, 'Mom, Jeff is dead! Susan killed him and buried him in the yard!'"

When Jeff's father, Ron Wright, got on the stand, he also recalled the fishy stories that Susan had told him during the week Jeff was missing. During a phone call the day after he disappeared, Susan told him and Kay that Jeff "had come back while she was gone, and taken his clothes and poured bleach all over her clothes.

"On Thursday she called and told us she'd had to pull up all the carpet and get rid of the mattress because of the bleach smell," Wright said.

The jury also heard testimony from the Wrights about Susan's erratic behavior in the days after Jeff was killed. How she'd taken his name off their joint checking account, how she'd held a garage sale and sold off some of Jeff's possessions, how she had re-taped the answering machine message on their phone to remove Jeff's voice.

Ron Wright also talked about Jeff's early relationship with Susan. Ron recalled how Jeff had called him after learning that Susan was pregnant.

"What was your fatherly advice, Mr. Wright?" Siegler asked.

"That the child needed a father," Ron replied. The answer left him shaken and Ron quickly broke down in tears, the only time that Friday that he would cry while testifying.

16

Jeff Wright's supervisor came in and testified that he was surprised and concerned when Jeff didn't show up for work on the morning of Tuesday, January 14, 2003. Kevin Conboy said that when customers kept calling and saying they were unable to reach Jeff, he finally began his own search for his co-worker.

Conboy said he'd taken a drive past the Wrights' house on January 15 and spotted Jeff's pickup truck parked in the driveway—but there was no sign of Jeff. When Conboy asked Susan what was going on, he got a variation of the story she was giving others—that they were having financial problems which had led Jeff to come home in a drunken rage and hit Bradley, so she had kicked him out of the house.

Conboy said he knew that Jeff had used cocaine in the past, but still he described his impression of Jeff's home life with Susan at that time as on the order of *Leave It to Beaver*.

"Did she seem angry?" Siegler wondered.

"She did not," Conboy answered.

"Did she seem to be afraid?"

"No, she did not," Conboy continued.

"Was she crying while she talked to you?" Siegler pressed.

"Never."

"Did she seem upset while she talked to you?" Siegler asked.

"No."

On the third day, Thursday, January 16, when once again Jeff didn't show up for work, Conboy made the decision to fire him.

The defense questions about cocaine use would come up again and again as each new witness took the stand. Davis and his co-counsel, Todd Ward, were quick to point out that some of Jeff's acquaintances knew about Jeff's faults and others didn't. The ones who did know bolstered Susan's case directly and the ones who didn't suggested there was a secret, darker side to Jeff Wright that might not have been obvious at first glance.

One of those who did know about Jeff's checkered history was his long-time friend Paul Cullen, who testified flat-out that Jeff was in the habit of cheating on Susan. Cullen said under oath that Jeff had been known to drive over to Austin to smoke crack and engage in three-way sex sessions with two strippers he knew. Cullen was also aware that authorities in Austin had once placed Jeff on probation for assaulting a topless dancer. His testimony made the point that there was concrete evidence that Jeff had been capable of physical violence against women.

That was reinforced by another witness that Friday, Erica Labian, a 29-year-old hair colorist at a salon that Susan frequented, when she testified that she had been troubled by a distinct bruise she had spotted on Susan's leg during a visit. "I thought she was being abused," Labian testified.

Davis and Ward also asked several witnesses to tell them what they knew about a trip that Jeff had made to Las Vegas. They noted that whatever he'd been up to in Sin City had resulted in him passing a sexually transmitted disease on to Susan upon his return.

17

Monday, March 1, 2004, would have been Jeffrey's thirty-sixth birthday, and the prosecution managed to slide that information in front of the jurors before the day was out; however, what would normally have been a day focused on Jeff was very much focused on Susan.

A juror who had fallen ill was replaced with an alternate by Judge Wallace. Then it was the defense's turn to put forward Susan's case in earnest.

Susan's defense was really self-defense, that she had acted to protect herself, and ultimately her children, against an abusive husband.

What self-defense cases turn upon are reasonableness and timing. Even a thoroughly rotten human being can legally kill someone in self-defense if they truthfully and reasonably believe that person is placing them, or another, under imminent threat of death or grave bodily harm. However, the crisis has to be severe and it has to be immediate. If the threat fades, even for a few moments, then it is no longer considered reasonable and lawful to use deadly force. If the victim has a window of opportunity and means to retreat, to escape, to call police, then they can no longer claim that taking lethal action was the only appropriate method of defending themselves.

Cases of justifiable self-defense usually arise in an instant and the legal opportunity to act in self-defense can also dissipate in an instant. Whatever happens before or after a killing where self-defense is claimed only becomes relevant, as it did in Susan's case, when it serves to provide circumstantial evidence as to the state of mind of the person *at the time* they resorted to lethal force.

In the land of pure legal theory, Susan actually arrived before the jury in a pretty good position. The legal burden was really upon the prosecutors to prove beyond a reasonable doubt that what she'd said happened wasn't true.

If Susan had in fact been raped by her husband and then opened her eyes to see him hovering over her with a knife, and if she had wrested control of it from him in a sudden burst of adrenaline-driven assertiveness—instantly turning the tables on a drug-addled overconfident bully with a few well-placed stabs—that probably would amount to a justifiable killing under the law.

Susan's problems centered on the evidence the state had collected during the autopsy, and the fact that her own actions in the minutes, hours, and days after the murder all looked bad, bad, bad. If she'd simply picked up the phone after stabbing Jeff and called 911, then it would have been a lot easier to believe her version of events.

If killing Jeff had been legally justified, then everything that followed it couldn't change that fact.

But if there were doubts about the justification—and, man, *were* there at the Harris County District Attorney's Office—then circumstances and context became hugely important.

If the jury couldn't see Jeff as an abuser, if there was no evidence that Susan had been raped or attacked that evening, if the medical evidence strongly suggested Jeff had been tied up before he was killed, if the burial of his body and the bleaching, painting, and cutting of carpets had been a frantic but failed cover-up attempt, then Susan was cooked. However, if the defense could show that much of what Susan had said about the circumstances surrounding the killing was true—that Jeff was abusive, that she had lived in fear for years, that he was starting to hit his kids, that he was high on cocaine when he died—then there was an opportunity to raise at least a reasonable doubt about whether or not a cold-blooded murder had really taken place on Berry Tree Drive.

At the start of the trial's second week, the defense team had to convince the jury—at least one member of it, anyway—that Susan was the cowering victim who had come out on top in a situation that she didn't start. If that were the case, then everything that followed that bloody outburst could be explained by a complete mental meltdown and confusion in the wake of a horrible incident. It was a tall order, and Davis got it under way by calling one of Susan's long-time friends and neighbors to the stand.

Sitting in the witness box in a bright turquoise blouse, Jamie Darr-Hall testified that Susan had told her she was being abused by Jeff.

"I didn't see abuse, but I saw bruises many times," Jamie testified, noting that on one occasion she saw Susan sporting a prominent black eye. At the time, Susan claimed it had been inflicted accidentally by her son.

While Susan held back tears, Jamie told jurors that she had seen Jeff abuse Bradley back when the boy was 2-and-a-half years old.

"It was very excessive, so it stuck in my memory. I witnessed him repeatedly spank Bradley in the course of about a half an hour," Jamie said.

Jamie had high praise for Susan's abilities as a mother, but she described Jeff as a cold control freak who had drug problems. She told the jury that she remembered Jeff trying to sell drugs to some teenagers at a friend's Halloween party one year.

Picking up on the issue of Jeff's excessive interest in control, Davis asked, "Was there ever an occasion where Jeff repeatedly called you?"

"Yes," she replied.

"Where was Susan when he called you?" Davis asked.

"She was driving in front of my house to her house."

"And how many times did Jeff call you?" Davis wondered. "In what period of time?"

"Four or five times . . . in about an hour," Jamie said.

"What did he ask you?"

" 'Where is Susan? Why is she not home?' " she replied.

Jamie said she spoke several times to Susan in the

days after the killing, when Jeff was still considered missing, and she remembered Susan crying and seeming very afraid.

Richard Darr-Hall also took a turn testifying. He recalled seeing Susan two years before at a school fund-raiser looking as though she had been beaten.

"She had a black eye, actually," he said.

"What did the black eye look like?" Davis asked.

"It was almost a half-circle around her eye. Kind of like someone had on the black stuff the football players wear," Richard said.

18

Next to testify was Susan's gray-haired mother, Susan Wyche, and she cut right to the chase, backing up Susan's claim that she was on the receiving end of a fiercely abusive relationship that she chose to hide from the world rather than confront.

Wyche said the abuse began before Jeff and Susan were even married, while Susan was pregnant with their first child.

"She said he was beating her directly in her stomach with his fist and she was screaming that he was going to hurt the baby, he was going to hurt the baby," Wyche said. "And she kept saying, 'What can I do, what can I do?' And I really didn't know."

Wyche said that during that time period, when she went to talk to Jeff about his behavior towards her daughter, "Jeff came outside and got within six inches of my face and hovered over me and began to scream at me and threaten me not to ever interfere with him or anything that he planned."

In the years that followed, Wyche said, there were

many times when she saw Susan with bruises, even with scars, and she assumed they were the product of Jeff's rages.

"I saw her with two separate black eyes. I have seen bruises on her legs," Wyche testified.

Wyche described the meeting with her daughter five days after Susan killed Jeff when she finally told her what had happened to him.

"I looked at her in desperation and I said, 'Susan, did you kill Jeff?' Thinking that anything short of that, we could handle it," Wyche said. "But her head just nodded forward and I thought, 'Oh!' "

Wyche said the afternoon took on a surreal tone from that point as she and Susan went with the two children to Target and Burger King before going back to the house and calling Neal Davis, asking him to come meet with Susan.

On her cross-examination, Siegler asked Wyche about something Susan had said to investigators when she first turned herself in.

"Ms. Wyche, isn't it true she told those people there that you were an abused wife of many years by your husband?"

"I've not seen her report, and I think that there are different ways of looking at abuse," Wyche replied quietly. "I don't look at my husband as an abusive person."

"Your daughters do, though, don't they?" Siegler pressed.

"Objection, Your Honor," Davis responded. "Speculation."

Judge Wallace let the question continue.

"My daughters grew up watching *Ozzie and Harriet* on TV," Wyche answered with a forced smile. "They saw *Leave It to Beaver*. We do not have that kind of a marriage, no. Nobody we know does."

19

An axiom of murder trial strategy is that it's not a good idea to put even the most innocent of defendants on the witness stand. Even people who have nothing to hide can come unglued when facing the slings and arrows of cross-examination. When someone's entire future hangs in the balance, few defense attorneys are willing to risk such an all-or-nothing play. However, Susan was in a unique position as a defendant. She began the trial by conceding about 90 percent of what was on the table at an average murder trial and she was pegging her entire defense on nuanced interpretations of the few remaining key details. That meant the jury would have to believe her. In the wake of Siegler's withering demonstration the week before, there was no way the defense team could risk leaving Susan's side of the story to the jury's imagination.

Susan's testimony would be remarkable not just because it was rare for a defendant to testify, but because it was literally the first official statement she had ever given about her case. Since she had "lawyered up" before the police investigation even began, she had never actually been interviewed by detectives. The authorities had prepared their case by gleaning what they could from Davis' comments to the press and by looking over the interviews they'd conducted with Susan's mother and sister in the days shortly after she confessed to the killing.

The prosecutors were completely confident that Susan was their killer, and they felt the forensic evidence from the autopsy provided overwhelming proof that this was a premeditated homicide, not some struggle for possession of a knife that resulted in death. That made the lack of a formal interview with Susan an inconvenience more than a problem, because whatever story Susan was going to tell about being a battered wife would have to overcome evidence that Jeff had been tied down when he was killed. Whatever the theory of the burden of proof, it was pretty clear that Susan would have to fight to convince the jury that things had transpired even remotely like she said they had.

And so, on Monday afternoon, exactly one week after it had started, the defense took their most significant gamble of the trial.

"Your Honor, the defense will call Susan Wright," Davis announced.

"Very well," Wallace replied.

With Susan finally on the stand, Davis began at the beginning. Susan, wearing a wide-collared pink shirt under the black blazer she had worn most of the trial, started calmly, almost timidly. She began by describing her life growing up in Houston as a "shy, quiet girl," who'd been a Brownie, and a peewee football cheerleader, and then a member of her church youth group.

She recalled meeting Jeffrey Wright in the spring of 1997 on the beach at Galveston. Jeff could be charming and attentive. He would bring Susan flowers and small gifts; he would take great care to arrange dates at nice restaurants; sometimes he would call her two and three times a day. The dates had rapidly evolved into a relationship, and in short order things had gotten a bit ahead of themselves. In 1998, at the age of 22, Susan had discovered that she was pregnant.

The clock was ticking and suddenly the successful young carpet salesman and the even-younger waitress had to make a monumental decision. Jeff talked about his desire to be a family man, how he pictured himself having a wife, a family, a house, even a dog. Susan loved Jeff and thought that was the track she was headed on as well.

Susan testified that the pregnancy was an oversight and it was not done to trap Jeff into a marriage. By the time they had decided to tie the knot—which was done in a small church in the town of Magnolia—she was eight months pregnant. It was a simple ceremony and they held their wedding dinner that night at the nearby Outback Steakhouse.

It was after the wedding and the birth of their son, Bradley, when the once considerate and kind Jeff turned 180 degrees and became in Susan's words, "a totally and completely different person."

"I had gained some weight," Susan explained. "So he told me what a fat-ass I was. He told me I was stupid and that I was worthless, and he said he knew why nobody liked me. He told me I looked like a beached whale."

Susan said that Jeff decided that he needed to have things done precisely his way around the house. In public, she was expected to support him, to put on a show of being "the perfect couple," but at home, out of sight of friends, family, and neighbors, Jeff demanded control over every aspect of their lives. Jeff had decided that everything that took place within their house was Susan's responsibility and that the place had to be spotless. Every domestic task, from cooking to the laundry, had to run like clockwork, and Jeff held Susan responsible for Bradley's appearance, demeanor, and behavior. If Bradley was cranky, it was Susan's fault. If things were running late, it was Susan's fault. He backed up his demands with accusations of infidelity on her part, even though Susan suspected that it was actually Jeff who was having affairs. He began to constantly belittle her appearance, her efforts, and her abilities, and then he began trying to control her with harrowing beatings.

Susan said the first beating came shortly after Bradley was born, when Jeff had come home with some marijuana and smoked it on the porch. After getting high on the pot, Susan said, Jeff wanted to pick Bradley up and bounce him around a bit, but it struck Susan as too much roughhousing for a tiny baby.

When she asked Jeff not to play with Bradley if he was high, Susan said, Jeff had exploded and threw her against a wall, grabbing her arms, shaking her, and punching her in the chest.

Susan called her sister, Cindy, the psychologist, and asked for advice. Hearing her sister crying and listening to what she had to say, Cindy at first told Susan that she would be right over to get her and Bradley. But Susan was terrified and told her not to come. The next day when Jeff was away, Cindy and her husband did arrive, packed up Susan's things, and took Susan and Bradley to her parents' house for the night.

The next morning Jeff showed up with a moving van to reclaim his wife and son. Susan returned home with him. It was the last time the Wyches would directly intervene in their daughter's marriage, but it would not be the last time Susan was beaten. In all, during the four years she and Jeff were married, Susan estimated she had been punched, kicked, or beaten approximately 150 times—about once every ten days.

Susan described one beating where she said Jeffrey had hit her repeatedly with a wooden ruler. After Davis asked her to show the jury where he'd hit her, she climbed down off the witness stand to present a demonstration of her own.

"What did he do?" Davis asked.

"He beat me in the back with it until it broke," Susan said.

"He hit you? How did he hit you?" Davis asked.

"First he hit me here in the back," Susan replied. "Then I covered myself, and he beat me all over on the back until it broke."

With Davis' help, Susan reenacted another attack that had taken place in her home.

"You said he shook you against the wall?" Davis asked.

"Yes," Susan replied.

"And what would hit the wall when he shook you?" Davis asked.

"My head and my entire back."

"Until his anger was done?" Davis wondered.

"Yes," Susan said.

"And then what did he do, you said?" Davis asked.

"He punched me in the chest," Susan replied.

"He punched you in the chest?" Davis repeated.

"Yes."

"He beat me," Susan said. We were in the computer room. "He punched me in the chest. He punched me in the head. He threw me down and kicked me in the back and in the legs until he wasn't mad anymore."

Susan said the worst beatings came when she had complained to Jeff about his drug use. She said one pounding came after she'd discovered a Baggie of marijuana in his pickup truck and flushed it down the toilet.

Jeff's most memorable attack was a kick to the stomach that had caused her to miscarry a pregnancy that was two months along.

Davis wondered what, if anything, Susan did to get help.

"I was embarrassed and I felt like it was my fault," Susan said. "I felt like if I could be perfect, he would be happy all the time and everything would be okay."

Susan said she had visited her doctor and he had prescribed some antidepressants, but when Jeff found out, he forbade her to take them. "He said they were for the weak," Susan testified. "He told me it isn't rocket science what women do, and that I should just suck it up."

On the one hand Susan was afraid of Jeff, on the other she loved him and kept thinking that if she could only be good enough, if she could just keep up with his requirements for perfection, things would eventually work out. It was a mind-set that in turn made her responsible for her own "failures" and rein-forced Jeff's notion that the core of the problems was that she was inadequate. If she just hadn't screwed up, he wouldn't have become angry in the first place.

According to Susan, the abuse, both physical and mental, was pervasive. Toys left on the floor would set Jeff off. Dinner taking too long would set Jeff off. Jeff could hit her one night and then force her to have sex against her will the next. His increasing use of cocaine just made him that much more edgy and pug-nacious.

Susan recalled an incident where she said Jeff taunted her with a friend's vicious pit bull and, when she expressed fear of it, he turned it loose. The dog promptly bit Susan and she showed the jurors scars that she said were from the attack.

Susan spent four hours on the stand describing an escalating series of beatings. First she was the victim, then the family dog, and finally her child, as Jeff got increasingly physical with Bradley and started punching him.

Divorce was out of the question. "He told me that if I ever left him that he would kill me, or he would take Bradley away to where I could never see him again."

Whenever Susan left Jeff's sight, when she traveled about the community during the day in her own car, Jeff would constantly wonder where she was and who she might be seeing, Susan testified. His paranoia over what his pretty wife might be up to bordered on the ludicrous. Susan described how Jeff had a developed a system of timing her visits to her parents' house so that he would be able to tell if she'd managed to slip out somewhere else, and presumably meet someone, during the trip.

"I was only allowed to stay for about an hour to an hour and a half," Susan said. "Then he would start to call and tell me that I needed to get home. When I went to the grocery store, if I stayed too long, he accused me of cheating on him with the bag boys."

The questions led inexorably to the night of January 13, 2003. Here, the questioning was picked up by Todd Ward, Davis's co-counsel.

Susan recalled Jeff coming home that night in an angry, aggressive mood. High on cocaine, Jeff's eyes were red and glassy. He had tussled with Bradley when the boy had refused to box, smacking his son in the face and causing him to come crying to Susan.

After the children were in bed, Susan waited for Jeff to get out of the shower before she confronted him, issuing what she described as an "ultimatum" that if he didn't start getting professional help for his drug use and anger issues, she was going to have no choice but to leave him. Susan remembered saying that she "couldn't take it anymore."

Susan said Jeff's response was instant and violent. He pushed her to the floor, kicked her over and over again in the stomach, and then dragged her into the bedroom and raped her.

Forced to have sex with her husband, lying on her own bed feeling that she'd just been violated, Susan said she'd had her eyes clenched shut when she suddenly heard Jeff muttering at her in an angry tone of voice.

"My eyes were closed and I heard his voice. It was scary. He said, 'Die, bitch!' and I opened up my eyes."

Looking up, Susan said she'd seen Jeff leaning over her with a hunting knife cocked back in his hand, a knife he had apparently pulled from a drawer in a bedside table. In an instant, Susan said, she knew that Jeff seriously intended to kill her this time. Thinking that she had only seconds to live, Susan said she decided it was now or never. It was time to fight back.

Springing up from the mattress Susan began clawing at Jeff. When she kneed him in the groin, she was able to gain the upper hand for a split second. "His grasp on the knife loosened just a little bit and I got it from him," Susan recalled.

"Why did you stab him?" Ward asked.

"Because I didn't want to die," Susan replied through tears. "He was going to kill me and I was scared. I couldn't stop.

"I threw my hands up and I grabbed the knife and I started kicking him with my right knee," Susan explained. "But it wasn't me. It was like I was watching it from above.

"I couldn't stop stabbing him," Susan continued ruefully.

"Where did you stab him?" Ward asked quietly.

"In his head, and in his chest, and in his neck, in his stomach, in his leg for when he kicked me," Susan answered, tears welling in her eyes. "I stabbed him in the penis for all the times he made me have sex with him that I didn't want to. I couldn't stop, because he was going to kill me. I couldn't stop because I knew as soon as I stopped, he was going to get the knife back and he was going to kill me. I didn't want to die."

Suddenly, Susan continued, there was a knock on her bedroom door and she stopped stabbing Jeff.

The already hushed courtroom went even quieter as the implications of what Susan had just said sunk in among prosecutors, jurors, and family members. This was the first time Susan had ever related this story, and it was clearly not something the observers had been expecting.

"Bradley was at the door," Susan said, drawing an audible gasp from the Wright family seated nearby.

Susan explained that she'd hurriedly put on her robe, hidden the knife, tied Jeff's right arm to the bed with a necktie to prevent him from getting up, and then opened the door a crack to let herself out into the hallway.

"So you put Bradley to bed . . ." Ward prompted.

"I walked him to his room, and I–I told him that everything was okay and to lay back down," Susan recalled. "And then I closed the door."

"So after you put Bradley to bed, then where did you go?" Ward wondered.

"I realized that I had left the knife in the room and I was scared," Susan explained. "I thought that I had to protect myself because he was going to come after me again. So I went into the kitchen, and I got another knife." She added that when she let herself back into the bedroom, she was still terrified that Jeff was going to rise up and attack her, so "I started stabbing him again."

Susan told the jury that she was already starting to slip mentally into a world where Jeff was both alive and dead, where little, if anything, made sense in the "fog" of emotions.

As Ward continued to walk Susan through the evening's events, she described her struggle to get Jeff's body off the bed and out onto the patio. She said she used the tie that had been holding him to the bed and another from a drawer to anchor his arms atop the metal dolly before wheeling him down the hallway.

"I took my bathrobe and I tied both of his ankles and then I tied him to the dolly so that he would stay on," Susan said. "I kept thinking that he was going to get up."

Even burying Jeff's inert body in the ground wasn't enough to convince Susan's shattered psyche that it was really all over, that he wasn't going to suddenly get up in a rage. Susan described to Ward the nights she spent awake on her living room davenport holding the knife and waiting for Jeff to return.

"He was still alive," Susan sobbed. "He was still going to try to come get me."

"I was afraid the second that I went to sleep he was going to come after me again," Susan said. "So I stayed awake and I watched."

"Why didn't you call the police?" Ward wondered.

"Because Jeff was still alive. My brain couldn't process it. There was no way that all the horrific, terrible things that happened in that room . . . My brain wouldn't let me accept that there was no possible way he was still alive." Her voice rose shrilly as she fought back tears, adding, "He was going to come back."

"You understand that's not rational," Ward responded.

"No, I understand that today," Susan answered. "But he was alive and he was going to come kill me."

What the prosecution had described as an obvious cover-up attempt was really a cleanup effort, according to Susan. Jeff had always been obsessed with having her keep a neat house and the massacre that had taken place had made a shambles of the bedroom. That was why she had set out in a frantic hurry to scrub, bleach, and repaint the damaged areas.

"I had to clean the house," Susan said. "It was so dirty and Jeff was going to be so mad at me anyway."

Even as the days began to pass, as she called relatives and told them tales of Jeff storming out, Jeff returning and bleaching the bedroom, even as she filled out police reports saying that Jeff was loose in the community somewhere and needed to be arrested, she herself was having great difficulty mentally processing the horror of what had just happened. She said she was still convinced that Jeff—who had dogged her every move for more than three years and exerted such a controlling influence over her—could still spring out of his hiding place and harm her again.

Describing what she could recall of cleaning out the joint checking account, changing the answering machine message, and holding a tag sale to get rid of some things, Susan said, "It's just things that I remember. The week was so foggy."

"You keep saying the same thing here, why is that?" Ward asked.

"Because he was alive."

20

The second Tuesday of the trial would be the last day—and in many ways the most crucial day—of the case itself.

Susan returned to the witness stand where she had spent three hours on Monday giving her version of the killing. This time it was Siegler who would be asking the questions. Even though these were the closing hours of the trial, this was still the very first opportunity the state had had to question Susan directly about what had happened fourteen months before. The day's schedule called for Susan to be cross-examined during the morning hours; for the afternoon session, both sides would present their final arguments to the jury. The previous afternoon Judge Wallace had instructed the jurors to come to court this day with their bags packed, because once jury deliberations began, they would be sequestered in a local hotel.

As Siegler got ready to take on the most important witness in the case, she was already convinced that Susan had tricked and bound Jeff, then tortured and slaughtered him when he couldn't move more than a couple of inches in any direction. Siegler was not prepared to give Susan even that much wiggle room.

Like the jury, Siegler had sat only a few feet from Susan as the defense offered its complex, often convoluted, theory of the killing, attempting to explain all the strange and alarming aspects of Susan's behavior, beginning with the night of the killing and continuing for the next five days. Susan was raped. Susan was terrorized. Susan was in fear for her life. Susan was able to wrest the knife from a coke-buzzed boxer in a flash of self-preservation. Susan snapped and couldn't stop stabbing him. Susan put Bradley back to bed and got another knife. Susan couldn't believe Jeff was really dead. Susan could call his parents and talk to them for over an hour and tell them a completely different story. Susan couldn't rationalize what had happened. Susan could bury the body in the patio and disassemble the bed. Susan was in a fog. Susan could show up and conduct a sincere-sounding set of interviews at Precinct 4 and swear out a warrant. Susan couldn't really process that Jeff wasn't still alive. Susan could get back and forth to Target and get all the cleaning supplies, paint, and bleach she needed to try to get rid of the crime scene and try to keep her story straight to Jeff's co-workers and their neighbors, etc., etc.

Siegler had heard the defense's explanation, and she had looked at the medical evidence. She had walked through the blood-spattered house and she had thought it over. She was convinced that there was a much simpler, more straightforward explanation for what had transpired over the course of that week in

January: Susan Wright had decided to murder her husband, she'd killed the SOB, and then she'd tried to get away with it. She couldn't cope with the difficulty of the plot that she'd set in motion, and after five days, the wheels had come off. Now Kelly Siegler had Susan Wright where she wanted her—right in front of twelve jurors who Siegler was confident would see things her way if they really just listened to what Susan herself had to say.

Siegler's biggest obstacle was that Susan didn't look like a killer. It may have been sexist, but a man in the same position explaining why he'd stabbed his wife 200 times, buried her in the back yard, and painted over the bedroom wouldn't have been believable. But Susan was a pretty woman, now 27 years old, with two young children, and when she wiped away tears and sat defensively in her black blazer in the witness box with her shoulders hunched, describing her husband bullying her, she was bound to generate sympathy for her plight. Siegler knew Susan's versions of events were riddled with inherent contradictions and she was determined to make Susan herself spell them out for the jurors, who would have to decide if they were plausible or the work of a scheming liar who was trying to trick them into letting her walk out the door.

Dressed in another of her trademark suits, this time dark blue with black velvet insets, Siegler began to bore in on the sides of Susan she wanted the jurors to see more clearly; she wanted to contrast Susan the mother of two with Susan the manipulative little stripper.

"How old were you when you were a dancer?" Siegler asked.

"I had just turned eighteen," Susan said, pausing a moment to think.

"At the age of eighteen, when you decided to become a dancer, would you agree with me that when you danced, you did so basically with no clothes on except a G-string?"

"We covered that yesterday, topless dancing," Susan reluctantly agreed.

"Is that a yes or a no, Ms. Wright?" Siegler pressed.

"Yes, ma'am. And it was only for two months."

"I didn't ask you that yet," Siegler volleyed back. "Was that a yes or a no?"

"It would be a yes," Susan reiterated.

Siegler wanted to know how it was that Susan could have been severely abused and beaten over the course of four years without ever having had her doctor notice that something was amiss. She pointed out that Bradley's teachers hadn't noticed any signs of abuse either. How come, Siegler wondered, when Susan went to see her doctor the very next day after she'd knifed Jeff, she didn't mention anything about having been forcibly raped the night before?

"He's a man, I wouldn't confide that in him," Susan replied.

"To your doctor?" Siegler asked incredulously.

"He's still a man, and that's still something that's extremely personal and embarrassing and . . ." Susan began.

Siegler cut her off. Referring to Susan's past antics

as a topless dancer, she interjected, "Miss, why did you dance half-naked for men for money? Don't sit up here and tell the jury you wouldn't tell your own doctor about something like being raped."

"It's the truth," Susan pouted. "That's something I kept to myself."

"You didn't keep your breasts to yourself," Siegler shot back.

Davis rose to object to the line of questioning. "She's charged with murder," he noted. "She's not charged with the things she did after the alleged offense."

Siegler pressed on, questioning whether there was any evidence—other than the testimony of a few witnesses—to prove that she really had been abused. After all, Jeff was physically much larger than Susan and if he had assaulted her full force over the years, he could have done a lot of damage.

"He would hit you as hard as he could and he would smash your head up against walls, dashboards, car windows, floors, all those things, but you never suffered any broken bones?" Siegler marveled.

"No, but I was in pain to where I could barely move," Susan replied.

Siegler simply didn't believe Susan, and she told her so. Siegler was convinced Susan was putting on a show for the jury, and that in fact, *she* was the one who had terrorized *Jeff,* at the point of a knife.

Picking up on Susan's version of events on the night of the stabbing, Siegler asked about the supposed confrontation with Jeff about his continuing drug use, a topic that she said had flipped him into a rage against her.

"That conversation never happened, did it?" Siegler said pointedly. "Because you were seducing your husband, getting ready to have sex with him."

Susan denied it.

Pressing onward Siegler wondered why anyone should believe Susan had been the victor in a struggle for control of a sharp knife when she was up against a man who was a hundred pounds heavier than her and was standing above her at the time.

"It was my sheer will to live," Susan said.

"Say that again," Siegler said, sounding as if she was rolling her eyes. "That was good. What did you say? 'My sheer will to live?' "

As she hammered Susan on point after point, Siegler would draw another small white card off a stack she had on the table in front of her, glance at it, and then slam the next query home.

"Here's a question for you: Did he scream?" Siegler asked.

"I don't remember any screaming," Susan answered with a shake of her head.

"You're stabbing him in the neck and chest and you don't remember any screaming?" Siegler asked in amazement. "Maybe that is because you don't want to tell this jury what he was saying. Like, 'Susan, what are you doing? Susan, please stop,' " she suggested.

"Here's a question for ya," Siegler said, her voice dripping in sarcasm. "When you stabbed him the fifty-sixth or the eighty-ninth or the one hundred and fifty-eighth time, was your arm getting tired?"

Susan cringed as the questions continued.

"To have a knife stuck in his chest, and his throat,

leg, and in his penis . . . How scary was it to Jeff, Mrs. Wright?" Siegler asked.

"Not scary, because he was going to do that to me," Susan replied.

"Why did you stab him in the eyes?" Siegler wondered.

Susan began hesitantly to answer, "Probably . . . I don't know . . ."

"Come on, Mrs. Wright," Siegler cajoled with a derisive edge to her voice, "why did you stab him directly in his eye? Can you say it's because you were that mad at him? Can you say it?"

"I wasn't that mad at him," Susan sniveled.

Siegler picked up a close-up photograph of Jeff's penis that had been taken during the autopsy and walked over to the witness stand to show it to Susan. Susan began to cry again as Siegler accused her of torturing Jeff.

"Do you feel the need to cry at the look of the penis that you stabbed, Mrs. Wright?" Siegler asked pointedly.

"How could someone not cry when they look at this?" Susan sniffled angrily.

"How can someone do that?" Siegler practically shouted back in response.

"Objection!" Todd Ward cut in. "She's arguing, Your Honor, with her."

Siegler then asked: "Did you hear the medical examiner testify that you didn't stab his penis? What you did was, you nicked at it . . ."

"No, I didn't . . ." Susan began to reply.

". . . and take little slashes at it?" Siegler continued.

"No," Susan said angrily. "I did not slash at him. No."

"You didn't stab his penis. That's not a stab like this." Siegler whammed her fist down on the front of the witness box in a stabbing motion, her voice rising to a shout. "Like you're mad, like you are afraid, like you can't, can't stop." Siegler hammered her fist down on the table with each word.

The display brought Ward right up out of his chair. "Objection, Your Honor, I'm going to ask the prosecutor to get back down in her seat, please, and refrain from doing this two feet from the witness."

"One more question," Siegler pushed.

"Have a seat," Judge Wallace admonished Siegler.

Smiling slyly as she prepared to walk back, Siegler goaded Susan once again. "That's a slice, isn't it?" she said, pointing to the photo in front of Susan.

"No," Susan glared back through teary eyes. "I did not sit there and nick at him. I did not do that. No."

"Is that a slice or a stab?" Siegler wondered.

"I don't know the difference . . ." Susan responded.

"Is that a nick or a stab?" Siegler continued relentlessly.

"I know that I stabbed at his penis, but I did not sit there and slice at him," Susan said angrily, her voice rising shrilly. "I did not do that."

"Yes, you did," Siegler shot back as she returned to her table.

"No, I did not. No," Susan said, shaking her head and covering her mouth with her hand as she began to cry.

Backing off just slightly, Siegler turned to the

disposal of Jeff's body under the patio, asking sarcastically, "What were your plans? Were you going to make a flower bed there eventually when people kind of forgot about Jeff?"

"There weren't any plans, because it didn't really . . . it hadn't sunk in that Jeff was dead, and that's where Jeff was," Susan answered. "Jeff was alive and he was still there. I kept, I was afraid that he was going to get up and come after me."

"And so you kept pouring dirt on him to keep him down?" Siegler prodded.

"I thought that I had to weigh him down because I was afraid that he was going to get up, and I knew that when he got up he was going to be very angry," Susan replied.

Siegler wanted to know why Susan thought any part of her story was believable—why anyone should trust her when she said things like she'd sat up night after night clutching a knife because she thought her husband was going to rise from the grave and come after her.

"I believed that Jeff was alive," Susan responded, with a tinge of resentment. "That wasn't a lie."

"And that's what you keep on telling us, isn't it?" Siegler continued. "That you thought Jeff was alive and he was going to come back and get you?"

"It's the truth. Yes," Susan said.

"And that fear kinda went in and went out during that week that he was cold and dead in that grave a few feet from your bed," Siegler continued. "Just like the fog kinda went in and out that week, didn't it, Mrs. Wright?"

"No. It was always there. I wasn't ever like totally coherent of what I was doing. I mean, there are things that I did that I always did, as far as taking care of the children and stuff like that. But the fear was there all week. There was no cover-up."

"There was no cover-up?" Siegler seized on the words.

"No, ma'am."

"What do you call paint?" Siegler pressed.

"It was cleaning," Susan said. "I thought it was dirt, and I had to make the house clean, because Jeff was going to be mad."

"That's right. In all the years of your marriage to Jeff, you always cleaned up the dirt with paint, didn't you?" Siegler said with palpable sarcasm.

"No, but the house was dirty and I had to make the house perfect," Susan replied.

Again, Siegler wondered aloud whether that was the best interpretation of Susan's actions, the explanation that made the best sense—or whether it was easier to believe that Susan was just plain lying.

Susan had talked to a lot of people in the wake of Jeff's death—his family, his co-workers, the neighbors, her doctor, her mother, her sister, the police department—and she didn't tell any of them what had actually happened. In fact, she told them several things that definitely didn't happen.

"You wouldn't lie to your mother?" Siegler asked demandingly. "Wouldn't lie to Jeff's mother? "Wouldn't lie to Scott Hall at Precinct Four? Wouldn't lie to your doctor? Didn't lie to all those people?"

"No, I wasn't lying," Susan answered.

"And you haven't told a single lie to this jury?" Siegler asked.

"No," Susan replied. "I believed Jeff was alive."

Siegler abruptly shifted her focus from the events of the previous year to Susan's demeanor during the trial the past week.

Referring back to Susan's reaction seven days before, when she had watched the prosecution's version of the stabbing re-created on the bed, Siegler asked, "And those flinches are real?"

"Those flinches are real because that is a scary thing," Susan replied. "Once that has happened to you, it's scary."

"Your lawyer, Neal Davis, put a piece of yellow paper in front of you and wrote on that paper in real big letters, 'CRYING,' And underneath it he wrote, '<u>BIGGER</u>,' and he underlined it," Siegler charged. "And isn't it true, Mrs. Wright, that all last week and through yesterday, when certain parts of the testimony would come out, you would begin to cry? Remember crying last week?"

"There were some very horrible, traumatic things," Susan replied in a measured tone.

"Absolutely. But every time the last man on this jury went through the door, you stopped those tears, didn't you?"

"That's not true," Susan responded. "I would put my head in my hands and I would try to compose myself because the judge asked me to."

"Did you not think that we weren't going to notice that every time the jury left the room, you managed to quit crying and get up and go chit-chat with your family and cut it up with your sister?" she wondered. "Did you think we weren't going to notice that, Mrs. Wright?"

"I wasn't cutting up with my sister," Susan responded in a hurt voice. "I was going there for support."

"And did you think that we weren't going to tell the jury how good you are at crying on cue and stopping crying on cue?" Siegler wondered.

"I haven't cried on cue once," Susan replied, dry-eyed. "Everything that I've felt was real. I don't see how someone could not cry throughout this."

"All those tears we saw yesterday were perfectly natural tears?" Siegler wondered skeptically.

"Those tears were real," Susan insisted.

Siegler wanted to know what had happened in the moments when Susan tied Jeff to the bedposts before the violence started.

"I did not tie him up," Susan said with a tinge of desperation.

"Oh, come on," Siegler urged. "You're a former dancer. There's nothing wrong with bondage. You're going to sit up there and tell this jury that you-all never practiced bondage?"

"Oh, no," Susan replied shaking her head in distaste.

" 'Oh, no,' " Siegler mimicked her. "That was good," she said, stretching the words for effect. "Are you, like, appalled at the idea? Is that where we get that 'Oh, no' from?"

Siegler shrugged off Susan's denial and through her mockery left the implication hanging in the air that Susan was just too prudishly embarrassed to tell the jury the truth. But the state actually had a lot riding on Susan's answer.

Frankly, if Jeff *wasn't* interested in being tied up that evening by Susan, then the state had no case. Because, as implausible as Susan winning a struggle for possession of a knife might be, there was simply no way she could have overpowered Jeff and methodically tied each of his limbs to a bedpost without his consent.

The bondage sex game was the core of the prosecution's theory. It was their basic explanation as to why Jeff's death was a premeditated murder and not a sudden struggle that could have gone either way. Yet it was a theory constructed entirely out of two pieces of circumstantial evidence and two inferences drawn from Susan and Jeff's personal histories.

The clearest pieces of circumstantial evidence that Jeff had submitted to being bound as part of a sex game were the neckties around his wrists.

In this era of kinky jokes on late-night TV and edgy soap operas, it didn't take long to imagine what might have been going on.

The thing was, the state didn't have one shred of evidence that the couple had actually done anything like that ever before. There was no admission from Susan. There was no drawerful of his-and-hers black leather underwear studded with metal spikes. There were no former lovers testifying that either Jeff or Susan had liked to get it on while tied up. In fact, the use of the neckties and the bathrobe sash had rather the opposite implication from the one the state was pushing. How many couples who were "into" bondage and had done this kind of thing over and over again would have used neckties as a restraint? Considering they cost at the very least about twenty bucks apiece, and can be wrecked with just a few seconds of stretching and straining, the state's theory would have actually been more convincing if Jeff had been tied up with just about anything else. Also, if Susan had been used to expertly tying and untying Jeff to the bed frame using neckties, why on this occasion did she cut them rather than untie them by hand? It couldn't have been because of the blood or the proximity to Jeff—the ties would have been the least of her problems on those two fronts that evening.

The other piece of circumstantial evidence, the trail of red candle wax dripped along Jeff's inner thigh, was the piece of the puzzle that made more sense when the state advanced the sex game theory. To bolster it, they had the fact that Susan had been a topless dancer and that Jeff liked to ogle—and then some—topless dancers; all of which left the implication dangling that if they were the kind of people who liked working and hanging out in clubs with a sexual theme, they were the kind of people who would be likely to tie each other up in bed.

It was curious, though, that when Siegler imagined the murder scenario for the jury, she visualized Jeff tied up in a bondage game, but never seemed to picture him as being gagged in the same instance. She'd asked Susan what words and phrases Jeff had screamed at her as she stabbed him 200 times, and Susan had testified that she didn't remember any screaming at all.

Susan had spent nearly three hours undergoing the

most intense cross-examination Harris County could throw at her. Siegler had asked her every hard question imaginable, grilled her on inconsistencies, questioned her honesty, mocked her sincerity, hung her up and left her to twist in the elements of her own story that had contrasted with her actions after the stabbing.

Closing arguments would begin that afternoon. By long-standing tradition, the party with the burden of proof would get the first and last word, so Neal Davis' last chance to raise a doubt in the mind of at least one juror would be followed by Siegler's rebuttal. Neither side was expected to take long. Susan's case may have been complex, but it wasn't inexplicably so, and there were only a few key elements of the evening of January 13 on which the two sides differed.

21

Davis began his closing argument by focusing on the state's theory of the motive. "Susan Wright has lived a nightmare for four to five years," he said, adding in an incredulous tone, "Someone is not going to stab someone else a hundred ninety-three times over a couple hundred thousand dollars. This was a brutal, terrifying, sadistic relationship that spanned years where Susan was just a mental and physical punching bag."

Davis questioned the scope and thoroughness of the police investigation. He argued that the paint Susan had used to cover the walls had also concealed makeshift patches on the holes in the wallboard that Jeff had made with his bare fists during frequent rages.

Again, Davis argued that Susan was the victim, not the aggressor, and that years of Jeff's abuse, intimidation, and controlling behavior had pushed her further and further off the foundation of her sanity until finally, after she had killed Jeff in self-defense, she had simply snapped and behaved strangely for less than a week until she got her act together enough to summon help.

"The moment you've got to focus on is when Jeffrey Wright was hovering over Susan with this knife," Davis urged. "He's the one that picked the fight. He's the one that picked the weapon. He's the one that picked the location. He picked the time. This is not some calculated, premeditated murder with two hundred stab wounds."

Susan had killed Jeffrey; Susan had eventually come forward and confessed; several witnesses had backed up Susan's claim that Jeff had battered, belittled, and oppressed her. She had been forced to do what any reasonable person would try to do when confronted with a lunatic with a knife—she had fought for her life, Davis argued. In the end, Davis said, Susan had no choice on the night of January 13.

Turning to the jury, Davis concluded, "It's time for y'all to put your foot down in this case. Enough is enough. Find Susan Wright not guilty. Let her get on with her life."

When it was the state's turn to present its closing argument, Siegler and Paul Doyle took turns making their key points—that Susan had done it and that Susan had done it on purpose and that every one of her justifications for doing it were out-and-out lies to avoid punishment for what she had clearly done.

Doyle pointed out that the only way anyone could stab her husband 193 times and bury him in the same house *and* escape prosecution would be to shift the blame onto the deceased.

"She's got to make Jeffrey Wright the most despicable, horrible, nastiest person that you could possibly imagine," Doyle charged. "He's a public urinator. He's a bed wetter. He's a cocaine user. He's a marijuana user. He's a dog beater. He's a child beater. He's a domestic abuser. Because she has got to sell you that."

Doyle and Siegler cast doubt on Susan's characterization of Jeff's demeanor that evening, noting that the only thing that anyone had to go on was Susan's word that Jeff was out of control. What if Jeff had just been "play-boxing" with Bradley that night? What if Jeff had never had possession of the knife? What if, as the autopsy clearly suggested, Jeff had been tied up and tortured? Then everything Susan said about that evening was a lie, and everything that followed in the next five days was every bit the cover-up effort that it appeared at the time.

"How long has she been lying? Since her arm got tired of plunging the knife in Jeff's body," Siegler said. "She's a good liar, and she's a good actress. Don't you forget it for a minute.

"She cries when you're in the room and she stops when you leave," Siegler told the jury, arguing that Susan had twisted the only facts she could get her hands on to come up with a scenario that would explain what had been done to Jeff. But when the evidence was examined the only proof was her word as the sole witness to events. Siegler thundered, "What you are left with is the word of Susan Lucille Wright—the word of a card-carrying, obvious, no-doubt-about-it, caught-red-handed, confirmed, documented liar.

"They tell you that their defense is self-defense," she continued. "No one really expects y'all to believe it's self-defense. But see, self-defense means you get to say 'battered wife.' And you get to say, 'Jeff's a jerk,' and 'Jeff's an abuser,' and [that] Jeff's all these horrible things.

"See?" Siegler quizzed the jurors. "That lets all that into evidence. You get it. And why is that all important?" Siegler wondered, answering her own question with a raised voice. "Because tomorrow, when we talk again, you won't care about Jeff being killed. This pretty little beautiful blonde lady won't be punished as severely because Jeff is such a jerk. Who cares about what happened to Jeff?"

Davis was back on his feet. "Your Honor, this is totally improper. This is punishment argument," he said, referring to the next phase of the trial.

"I'm talking about their strategy, Judge," Siegler responded.

Wallace quickly overruled the objection, motioning for Siegler to continue.

"That's what's going on here," she assured the jury.

"The purpose of that bed we brought out here was to freeze in your mind forever the image of how helpless and weak and defenseless Jeffrey Wright was as this defendant stabbed him over and over again," Siegler said.

Siegler summed up with the reasons why she thought Susan was on trial as a murderess. She described a scene in which both Jeff and Susan were nude and Susan had tied him up—Siegler was sure Susan had done so many times before. She said it had all the makings of a great romantic evening at home, where Jeff was the most vulnerable. "She was setting the mood, she was teasing him, she was leading him on, she was getting him aroused. She was kissing him, licking him. She was flirting with him and loving him for all she was worth. And at some point, when the wax was melted just enough, she poured a little bit on his penis." Siegler nodded at Susan, then continued: "She turned that bedroom into a torture chamber. She turned that bed into a butcher block."

22

With that it was time for the seven men and five women on the jury to begin discussing the fate of Susan Wright.

Judge Wallace had anticipated a two-week-long trial, and so far it had run a week and two days. It was those last two days—featuring the direct testimony from Susan, and Siegler's witheringly caustic cross-examination—that were still hanging in the air as the jurors filed out of the courtroom at 3:30 P.M Tuesday afternoon to commence deliberations.

Trying to guess what a jury might be thinking is purely a fool's errand, but it's something that all sides—and especially reporters—try to do to fill the void while they have to wait. In the Wright case, however, it was clear from the seven working days the trial had run so far that there was really only one central issue in this entire case: Either Susan had tied up Jeff *before* she started stabbing him, or she hadn't.

It had already been a long, draining day, so after two hours of getting situated, the jury decided to call it an evening. They left the courthouse and headed for the downtown hotel where Judge Wallace was planning to have them sequestered for however long it took to reach a verdict.

Susan and her family headed home and their nervous wait continued.

At 8:30 A.M. on Wednesday, the deliberations resumed and had been under way about an hour when a message came down from the jury foreperson to the court. Messages containing questions from the jury are usually the only clues court watchers have to divine what a jury is thinking or how far it's progressed in its deliberative process, but while this request from the Wright jury was intriguing, it was also utterly cryptic as far as what it did, or in this case, didn't reveal about their thinking.

The jurors wanted to know if they could again see the bloody bed. It was an exhibit that was properly in evidence, so normally such a request wouldn't even have raised an eyebrow. The only issue with the bed was how to make it available. It was simply too large to be carried in and set on the middle of the conference table in the jury room with all the other exhibits.

Judge Wallace decided to have the bed set up once again in the middle of the courtroom, and uniformed deputies hauled in the pieces and reassembled it. The jurors filed back in to silently gaze at it for a few minutes. Then, apparently satisfied, they returned to their conference room and continued.

Attorneys and observers were just starting to make plans to leave for lunch when, at 11:30 A.M., word came down that everyone should quickly gather in the courtroom. In all, the jury had only taken five hours to reach a verdict on the death of Jeffrey Wright.

23

Both sides waited at their desks for the jurors to file in and take their seats. Susan, who had spent much of the week cringing and weeping, was now remarkably calm.

As her mother and sister waited nervously behind her, Susan turned to her mother and said in a quick whisper, "It's okay." Then she turned back to watch Judge Wallace take the written verdict form from the jury foreman. Rising to their feet, Susan and her attorneys appeared stoic as Wallace looked at the form for a moment and began to read.

" 'In the *State of Texas* vs. *Susan Lucille Wright*, we the jury find the defendant, Susan Lucille Wright, guilty of murder as charged in the indictment,' " Wallace read. "It's signed by the foreperson of the jury. Thank you. You may be seated."

Susan stared straight ahead and did not react. Behind her, her sister Cindy bit her lip. Davis immediately rose and asked Wallace to confirm the verdict. "Poll the jury, Your Honor."

The polling of the jury—to acknowledge that this

was indeed the opinion of each member—went swiftly and mechanically.

Wallace thanked them again and announced that after lunch, both sides would begin their arguments for the sentencing phase of the trial.

Even before the sentencing phase had begun, experts watching the trial were speculating about the appeal that would inevitably be filed, as they always are in high-profile cases. The first thing that leapt out as potential grounds for arguing that the trial had been unfair to Susan was Siegler's demonstration on the bed.

The basic legal rule was that anything that Siegler could legitimately describe in front of the jury, she could also demonstrate for them, as long as the words she was using matched the moves she was making. However, Siegler herself had demonstrated the limits of that concept when, a few minutes after she'd straddled Doyle with the knife to demonstrate the stabbing, Judge Wallace had prohibited Doyle from sitting on top of her to demonstrate how difficult it would have been for Susan to have gained possession of the knife from Jeff.

The issue at stake was one both of taste and of prejudice. Propriety isn't really much of an issue when you are discussing something as deadly serious as how a human being got a knife stuck in them 200 times, but there is an issue of fairness involved when prosecutors vividly present something that they are really inferring from circumstantial evidence. It's up to the jury to decide whether something is plausible or not and, for the same reason that the Securities and Exchange Commission prohibits stockbrokers from aggressively enticing investors with advertisements of all the yachts, sports cars, and other goodies someone could buy if they struck it rich in the market, prosecutors are generally not allowed to play-act crimes, because there's a danger the acting job can override the facts. Demonstrations, however well intended, also run the risk of inadvertently filling in little details between moves where there isn't actually testimony to support the actions depicted.

Since the Wright case was being covered by a number of television networks, it was only a matter of minutes after the jury reached its decision that reporters and analysts began questioning whether the case would be appealed on the grounds that Siegler's on-the-bed demonstration had been overly vivid.

"It's one thing to present your theory and argument to the jury, your version of what happened, but this was inflammatory and over the top," CNN legal analyst Kimberly Guilfoyle Newsom said in one such segment that was seen literally around the world. "I don't think anyone can say with a straight face that this wasn't prejudicial to the defendant in this case. This was [the prosecution's] rendition of what happened. They laid the whole thing out for the jury. I think the jury bought it hook, line, sinker that this is exactly what happened."

24

After a break for lunch the sentencing phase of the trial began, but outside on the steps of the courthouse legal analysts and reporters were already facing television cameras from across Houston, and across the country, and predicting that the kind of jury that would convict Susan in five hours flat was probably the kind of jury that was going to put her behind bars for the rest of her life. This was, after all, Texas. It might not always be the law-and-order state, but it sure as heck had a reputation as the punishment state.

With the admitted benefit of 20/20 hindsight, however recently acquired, the analysts were also busy saying that the guilty verdict against Susan had been something of a slam dunk.

The one feature of the case that stood out was simply the number of times Susan had stabbed Jeffrey. No matter how nuanced her explanation, no matter how "out of it" she'd been mentally at the time, the notion that she'd stuck a knife in her husband upwards of 193 times was enough for the public to comfortably write Susan off as a murderer and not a defenseless victim.

Back in the courtroom the two sides resumed their familiar places and began to argue whether or not Susan should spend the rest of her life behind bars.

It had been an emotional trial up to this point, but now there was no longer any reason for Judge Wallace to admonish those testifying to restrain their feelings. This phase of the proceeding wasn't about the cold facts of knife angles and time-lines. This was about Jeff and the gut-wrenching hole that his death had blown through two families and the lives of over a dozen people who loved him.

"I have nightmares," Jeff's sister Terry Roberts told the jury. "I see her eyes. Those evil, empty eyes."

Jeff's father, Ron Wright, Sr., was one of the most powerful witnesses, describing Susan as the biggest liar he'd ever encountered, and then sobbing as he spoke from the witness box about how the past year had affected his family when they thought about what Susan had done to their son. "Unbelievable. I mean, how can a human being do what she did to our son? Stab him in the eyeballs while he's awake? I can't believe he's dead. I can't believe she did it. She's evil!" he cried, his cheeks wet with tears.

As Wright continued, saying that Susan was simply lying when she said that Jeff had been abusive towards her, it was Susan's turn to begin crying.

When it came her turn to speak, Kay Wright said matter-of-factly, "It's been the worst year of my life."

After a family court judge had discovered that Bradley and Kaily were living with Susan, and not with Cindy Stewart, custody was switched to the Wrights and eventually to Jeff's older brother Ron, Jr. and his wife.

It had been an awkward situation for all of the Wrights, because Susan still had visitation rights while her court case was pending, and she'd been allowed to travel to Austin each weekend to spend time with the children.

Taking the stand, Ron Wright, Jr. testified, "Our immediate concern was for the children. We're with the children." He described the past months of caring for Bradley, who was now 5, and Kaily, who was now 2. Ron, Jr. said that he and his wife were planning to adopt the pair now that Susan had been convicted. As he spoke of the decision that he and his wife had made to adopt his brother's children, several jurors began wiping away tears. "We feel we're the best shot that they have to have a normal life," Ron, Jr. said.

All of the Wrights had argued for the maximum possible punishment. When it came time to hear from Susan's family, they argued just the opposite—that she should be placed on probation so her children would not have to be separated any longer from their mother. "Susan is the sweetest, most tender-hearted person I've ever known," Susan Wyche told the jury. "You would never, ever, ever have suspected that Susan could commit an act like this."

Wyche urged the jurors to give her daughter the lightest possible sentence, which would be probation, in order not to cut her off from her son and daughter. "She'll never miss a moment with those children." Wyche implored. "They are her life."

"Do you think Susan Wright could be a good candidate for probation?" Davis asked.

"She's very responsible," Wyche answered.

Susan broke down and cried some more as she listened to her mother and sister speak on her behalf.

After the families had testified, Judge Wallace glanced at the clock and called it a day. The sentencing hearing would resume on Thursday morning. That would feature closing arguments from the attorneys once again—and once again Kelly Siegler would have the last word before the jury decided Susan's fate.

Whatever the jury eventually would decide about the length of her imprisonment, the fact was that Susan now stood convicted of murder, and this night she would have to begin serving her sentence in jail. She left the courtroom in the custody of constables.

25

On Thursday, the attorneys made their arguments, and Susan watched, arms crossed, from the defense table. She wore the same clothes she'd appeared in the day before. Spending her first night in jail as a convicted felon, she had no way to arrange for a different outfit for this part of the proceedings.

Davis tried mightily to get the jury to believe that Susan deserved consideration because she had been the victim of abuse. It was a bit of a strange case to be making when the same jurors had just rejected that argument as an explanation for Jeff's killing, but it was really the only argument the defense had ever had at its disposal.

Davis reminded the jury of the testimony, even from Jeff's friends, that he was someone who snorted cocaine, becoming mean and paranoid when he did so. Again Davis brought up the fact that, even though it hadn't been overwhelming, the only abuse prior to the stabbing that anyone had testified to appeared to have been directed at Susan and not the other way around. Davis urged the jury to consider what it would have been like for her to live in terror that Jeff was going to fly into a violent fit and beat her.

"The cause of this case was Jeff coming home on cocaine, Jeff beating Bradley, and Jeff beating Susan," Davis said.

Davis held up photos of Susan, showing bruises that he said were inflicted by Jeff.

"It isn't throwing mud on Jeff" Davis practically pleaded. "This is showing you his predisposition toward violence, to show you what Susan was dealing with. He was stabbed nearly two hundred times. If ever there were a crime of passion, if ever there was a crime of terror, if ever there was a crime of desperation, this is it!"

Putting up pictures of Susan with her two young children, Davis argued that, despite what she had gone through, despite what she had done, she had always been a good mother, and deserved the lightest possible sentence so she could continue to be with them.

"We respectfully ask that she get probation in this case," Davis concluded. "That is the right, fair, and just thing to do."

Probation was the last thing the prosecution thought Susan deserved after she'd tied her husband up and slaughtered him.

"You'd be patting her on the back and saying, 'Susan, go on out there and try to cut down on that killing,'" Assistant District Attorney Murray Newman told the jury.

When it became her turn, Siegler, standing in a dark pink suit jacket, invoked the honor of Texas as grounds for giving Susan the max. Pointing out the television cameras that were broadcasting what went on in the courtroom to the entire country, Siegler put it on the line for the jurors: "You want all those people out there to think that a Texas jury gave a Texas woman probation for stabbing her husband a hundred and ninety-three times?"

Siegler urged another outcome: at least 45 years behind bars. The prosecutors wanted to ensure that Bradley and Kaily would both be adults before Susan was even eligible for parole.

Taking the self-defense and domestic abuse arguments head-on, Siegler told the jury to ignore any attempts to inveigle their sympathies on the grounds that Susan was really the victim here.

Picking up the knife that had been entered into evidence, Siegler began to make overhand stabbing motions at the table. "When you take this knife and then you count it one hundred ninety-three times with this knife—Count it," she urged, continuing, "One, two, three, four, five, six, seven, eight, nine, ten, eleven, twelve, thirteen, one hundred ninety-three times." Her voice seemed tinged with awe at the enormity of it. "Do you know how long that would take? You would have to take a rest to finish it up."

"Sudden passion? It was all a big old lie so that y'all would feel sorry for her and think that Jeff was a big old brute," Siegler said, her Texas accent picking up speed as her voice rose. "Their defense strategy has always been that Jeff deserved killing, so his killer doesn't deserve punishment.

"The fact she has pretended to be a battered wife is disgusting. This woman has hurt the cause of truly abused women, because her lies and manipulations have caused a lot of people to be more skeptical next time some woman who was really abused walks into a police station.

"People go to prison for one stab wound," Siegler said. "She did hundred ninety-three of them, to his death."

With the brief closing arguments concluded, it was once again time for the jury to retire and deliberate Susan's fate. Judge Wallace read the jurors a series of instructions, informing them that because Susan had gone twenty-seven years without any prior criminal record, she was indeed eligible for a strictly probationary sentence, if they so decided.

At 10 A.M. the jury filed out. This time, based on the speed of the conviction the previous day, the expectation in the hallways was actually that the decision would come swiftly. When it came mid-afternoon, it was a bit of a surprise that the jury had taken just over five hours, nearly the same time it took to decide the question of Susan's guilt.

26

It was just after 3:30 P.M. and Susan shook visibly as
the jury foreman passed the group's written decision
up to the bench. Judge Wallace paused just a moment
to check it before he looked up and read: " 'We the
jury, having found the defendant guilty of murder, as-
sess her punishment at confinement in the institu-
tional division of the Texas Department of Criminal
Justice for twenty-five years,' signed, the foreperson
of the jury."

On one special-issue question of sudden passion,
the jurors had been asked, "Will you, the jury, find by
preponderance of the evidence that the defendant
caused the death of Jeffrey Wright under the immediate influence of sudden passion arising from an ade-
quate cause?" The jury had answered "No." If they'd
decided sudden passion had been a factor, then they
would have automatically been limited to a 2- to 20-
year sentencing range.

Susan began quietly crying. When Wallace asked
her, "Is there anything you wish to say at this time?" she

silently shook her head. Behind her, her sister Cindy began to sob openly.

It was impossible to tell what was going through Susan's mind, because the sentence, although lengthy by any standard, was actually one of the lesser punishments that the jury could have imposed.

Under Texas law, Susan would be eligible for parole in half of the maximum time—which in this case meant she could walk out the door of the correctional center in as little as 12-and-a-half years. Depending on how she fared with her parole board in the future, she would be between 39 and 52 years old when freed. Hardly a picnic, but nothing like the maximum of 99 years behind bars, or even the 45-year minimum that the prosecution had fought for.

As the constables began to lead Susan back to prison, she turned to her mother, father, and sister and, putting her hand up to her mouth in anguish said simply, "I'm sorry."

After Susan had left, Judge Wallace afforded Ron Wright, Jr. the opportunity to read a brief victims' impact statement to those who remained in the courtroom.

"The last words Jeff Wright ever spoke to his family were, 'I love you, Mom,'" Ron, Jr. began reading. "Jeff's life was taken from him by someone who had no right to take it. The only one that can take a life is the ultimate Creator of life itself. Jeff Wright cannot stand before you today that you may judge for yourselves the kind of person he was. Jeff Wright was tortured to death by Susan Wright in a selfish, senseless manner. We are his voice now. Jeff Wright loved life and all those who are a part of his life. He was not the monster that some have chosen to say he was. Jeff Wright was a son, a brother, a husband, father, and a friend. Many are those who are blessed by his life."

Outside the courtroom on the steps of the courthouse, the media had gathered once again to see the final chapter of the case. The yin and yang effect of the quick and decisive verdict of guilty, followed by what, for Texas at least, seemed a light sentence for such a savage crime, genuinely caught legal experts off-guard.

"I was surprised," admitted Professor Gerald Treece, a legal analyst for KHOU 11 News, in an interview immediately after the announcement. "I thought she would get upwards of forty-five years. She tortured this guy. Twenty-five years for killing your husband is not that harsh of a sentence."

27

It had been a long week-and-a-half for everybody involved in the trial, but the hardest lot had unquestionably fallen to the five women and seven men who had served on Susan Wright's jury.

Legal theories and esoteric arguments are one thing, but the jurors had to watch and weigh every nuance, look at hideous and upsetting photographs, endure cathartic tearful testimony from fathers, mothers, siblings, and close friends from both sides—all the while knowing that, no matter what decision they reached, in the end they were going to deeply hurt at least one branch of Bradley and Kaily's families and in some sense alter those children's lives forever.

By law and by tradition, jurors are not required to account in any way for how they reached their decisions. Following a trial the details of their deliberations can either be as secret, or as open, as the jurors themselves wish. Thus, reporters always feel a deep sense of gratitude when jurors do come forward and speak with the press, especially after complex cases that have been closely followed by the public.

Shortly after the courtroom cleared out, word came down to reporters that several of the jurors would be willing to speak on the record. The press corps quickly reassembled in the courtroom, where a podium had been set up.

Although nine of the jurors showed up for the hastily assembled press conference, only the men on the panel ended up speaking to reporters. They assured the gathering that it was just a question of who felt comfortable in the media spotlight, not a sign that there had been an internal split along gender lines during the deliberations.

The jurors provided an interesting look into their thought process during both the guilt phase and the sentencing phase of the trial.

Even though the prosecution had painted Susan as a conniving schemer out to kill Jeff for money and then con a jury into releasing her, and even though the defense had portrayed Susan as nothing more than an innocent victim to the point that she had suffered a mental breakdown, the jurors seemed to have landed in a middle ground that both sides had denied even existed. Namely, they said they had discounted the prosecution's theory of the motive and believed Susan's claims of an abusive relationship, but at the same time they didn't believe Susan had acted in self-defense on that particular night.

"I think what we came to was, Mr. Wright was not a model husband," juror Ed Domangue told the press.

"The extent of abuse was not something we were able to challenge."

"Do you believe he beat her that night?" asked a reporter.

"No," Domangue replied.

The jurors said they had been impressed with how normal Susan seemed, how she could have been someone they passed at the mall or met at the PTA or saw at their jobs. They said they'd tried to give her the benefit of the doubt that she was entitled to, even though there had been a clear difference of opinion around the jury table as to just how bad a spouse Jeff might really have been.

But in the end, even those who were prepared to believe the worst about Jeff shared the same questions about the claim of self-defense. It had all come down to the question of whether or not Jeff had been restrained when Susan began stabbing him. Her claim to have wrested a knife away from an angry 220-pound man who had just raped her just didn't seem plausible. And then there were the ties around Jeff's wrists. If Jeff had been tied down when she stabbed him that first time, then, the jurors said, it just couldn't be construed as self-defense.

"For me, it was the ligatures," juror Brian Knight explained. "The way they were tied was the biggest factor we had . . . how these ligatures affected him if he was tied down or not."

"I personally did not find her credible," jury foreman Dale England added. "There were too many holes in her story."

Juror Dave Belding echoed that sentiment, saying that putting Susan on the witness stand had been a mistake after all. She had looked like she was following a coached script. "She said, 'He would kick me and kick me until he wasn't angry anymore.' It was not only the same words, but the delivery, if you will."

Jurors explained that the reason they'd asked to see the bed reassembled during the deliberation was that they had been intensely studying the photographs of the knotted neckties back in the jury room and needed to convince themselves that Jeff had really been tied down.

Still, as they discussed the various details, they were never able to arrive at what they thought the real motive for the stabbing was. The question of what had driven Susan to stick a knife in Jeff all those times was never answered.

"I don't think any of us are going to, anytime soon, understand that," Ed Domangue noted.

Juries aren't obligated to deduce the motive before they convict someone, they just have to believe beyond a reasonable doubt that the crime was committed and that the person accused did it. The question of why anyone kills somebody is really one of those unfathomables that quickly leaves the realm of the everyday and skates into the land of psychology and perhaps even religion and metaphysics.

The decision to give Susan a relatively light sentence had been something of an averaging out of opinions between those jurors who believed that Susan had been severely abused and those who didn't. The actual sentence being contemplated by individual jurors when the deliberations began ranged from less than 25 years clear on up the scale to the maximum.

"The way we arrived at the twenty-five years was just a systematic discussion around the table," Domangue explained. "We ironed out our differences. We made compromises."

In the hours and days that followed, some of the jurors, as well as Neal Davis and Kelly Siegler, made appearances on a number of local and national television shows to discuss the case. The headline that the woman who'd stabbed her husband 193 times had finally been convicted by a Texas jury was in papers across North America, Europe, and Australia.

"Frankly, in our deliberations, we never really thought that life insurance was a motivator," juror Dave Belding explained on Fox News, adding, "We tried to be as sympathetic as we could to her situation as an abused spouse trying to raise the children. A lot of the evidence that came in that disparaged Jeff Wright had to be filtered appropriately. Some of it we thought was a little over the top, but clearly he was not a Boy Scout, at least in our assessment. And again, sympathies will get you so far, but with the factual evidence and the sequencing of events, we couldn't get to the point we needed to be comfortable with her acting in self-defense."

Asked if he thought Wright had been believable when she testified, Belding replied, "I think there were many parts of her testimony that I personally viewed as very compelling and, again, found her to be a sympathetic character. There were other parts of her testimony that unfortunately I found to be a bit melodramatic, and what I personally viewed to be rehearsed. Again, I'm not suggesting that's inappropriate. Just, it didn't stand the test of my view of credibility. And one other comment that I would just make for the benefit of my fellow jurors, we all ultimately had to get over the hurdle that [Susan said] Mr. Wright had not been bound and tied up with the ligatures that were present on his body at the time he was removed from the grave," Belding concluded.

Neal Davis appeared on CNN in the midst of what had been nearly non-stop coverage of the other big trial under way in the nation, the Martha Stewart case in New York.

Asked what he thought the jury had gotten wrong, Davis replied, "Well, I think you have to look at the hard evidence in this case. And the facts of the case showed that the deceased had defensive wounds on his hand and that Susan had defensive wounds on her hands. And that's exactly what prosecution, not defense witnesses, testified to," Davis said, continuing, "I think that casts serious doubt on whether he was tied up. If he was tied up in that bed, then he would not have gotten defensive wounds on his hands. The defensive wounds suggest that there was some struggle over the knife. And that was what we said all along."

Kelly Siegler also took a turn in the media spotlight, telling Houston's KHOU 11 News that Susan Wright's trip to the witness stand had been her own undoing. "She is a liar, and it is hard not to catch a liar who is lying," Siegler said. "You can't keep that up for two hours, especially when you tell as ridiculous a story as she did, locking herself into all those crazy details." Siegler added that if Susan really had been the victim of sustained and severe abuse, somebody somewhere would have seen more concrete evidence of it.

Ever since 1893, when a jury in Fall River, Massachusetts, gave Lizzie Borden a pass on the murder of her father and stepmother, there's been a lingering question of whether women who kill are treated differently from men.

Harris County has a formidable reputation as the number one spot in the nation to seek, and get, the death penalty in heinous murder cases. But almost without exception, the defendants were male. When Andrea Yates drowned her five children in a bathtub, a Harris County jury rejected the notion that she was insane, but they declined to sentence her to death, opting for life in prison instead. When crazed dentist Clara Harris ran over her cheating husband with her Mercedes, the jury decided she'd killed him deliberately, but gave her only 20 years. Now Susan had plunged a knife into her husband a record-breaking number of times, and a jury had concluded she'd done it deliberately, but still only sentenced her to what amounted to 12 to 25 years behind bars.

There was some grousing after the trial about the length, or brevity, of Susan's sentence, depending on which side the observers fell on. Two points seemed to stand out in the wake of the jury's decision: first, those who supported Jeff's side of the equation argued that if things had been different and Jeff had stabbed Susan a couple of hundred times, then he would have almost certainly gotten the maximum; second, those who believed Susan was a battered woman who'd finally fought back wondered why the phrase "former topless dancer" was being brought up every time her name was mentioned, when it apparently had nothing to do with the killing.

28

Susan spent the first few days after her conviction in the Harris County Jail, but she was soon transferred to the tiny central Texas town of Gatesville, which is only about twenty miles from President George W. Bush's ranch in Crawford.

The women's prison in Gatesville is really a campus of the main facility and several smaller "satellite" prisons scattered in and around the town that together house Texas' vast collection of female prisoners. In 2003 the prison population in Texas included 13,487 women, about a third of whom were in for drug offenses. It's the largest population of women prisoners in the country—more than California, more than the entire female federal prisoner population.

Susan's conviction had her attorneys searching for grounds to appeal, but it also set up another legal confrontation—one with her in-laws over custody of her young children.

Clearly if Susan was going to jail for one or more decades, then the children needed a home. The temporary custody that had been awarded to Ron Wright,

Jr. and his wife in Austin would not be good enough.

When the Wrights had moved for full custody through an outright adoption in Harris County's family court, they also asked that Susan's parental rights to Bradley and Kaily be completely severed. That would mean that Susan would lose even the legal right to have visitations with them, something she was prepared to fight for even from behind bars.

"I will go broke trying to keep these children from seeing their mother in prison," vowed Ron Wright, Sr. in an interview with the *Houston Chronicle*.

The final decision will be up to a judge, not the relatives, and it is fairly common practice for women who are incarcerated to have visits from their children in jail—just as they would with any other visitor in a designated visiting area within the facility. Whether those visits take place through a thick pane of glass or involve "contact" depends mostly on the individual prisoner's history of disciplinary problems in the facility, rather than the charges on which she was convicted.

Bradley was attending a Christian pre-school in Austin as hearings on the custody issues approached in the summer of 2004. Susan had not seen the children at all in the months following her conviction, but she was writing them letters in care of her sister in the hopes that Cindy could read them to her nephew and niece when they were old enough to understand. One of them read in part, "I feel when I came here I was a caterpillar. This is my cocoon and metamorphosis, with God's help, will allow me to fly out of here a beautiful butterfly. I miss you all."

29

For murder defendants a conviction is not usually the end of the legal road, and as Susan headed off to prison, efforts were already under way to appeal her case.

As Susan had stated during her testimony, she and Jeff were having financial problems at the time she killed him. Now, over a year later, the extraordinary costs of her legal defense had left her destitute. It meant that she was no longer able to hire the services of Neal Davis, Todd Ward, and their top-flight law firm.

Instead Susan filed paperwork with Harris County declaring that she was indigent and would need a publicly appointed lawyer to carry out her appeal. It was a right that she could exercise, and for which Harris County was prepared to shell out about $5,000, but it also meant Susan would have to take the luck of the draw as to who was assigned her case from Houston's rotating bar of public defenders.

In mid-March, Wright's application was granted and her appeal was assigned to Kenneth McCoy, who had a decade of experience as a defense attorney. Hours after his assignment, McCoy told the *Houston Chronicle* that he had seen some of the press coverage of the case, but knew few of the details. "I'll handle it like any other appeal," McCoy told the paper.

After a weekend meeting with Susan in her jail cell, McCoy told reporters that he was indeed going to concentrate on the "over-the-top" demonstration Siegler put on with the bed in the courtroom as one of the main grounds for the appeal.

The bed itself was kept in a back hallway behind Judge Wallace's courtroom. It had remained there for a week after the trial concluded, and then Wallace ordered that it be destroyed along with its mattress and box spring. Wallace had a court photographer document each of those components first so if Susan won the appeal and another trial were held, there would be photographs to show how the pieces had looked.

Siegler told reporters that if her reenactment of the stabbing was the best grounds that the defense had to try to gain a new trial, then, "We're looking pretty good."

Siegler had argued all along that if she was permitted to bring the actual knife into court and show it to the jury, then she should be allowed to bring in the actual bed, since the way she thought it had been employed made it every bit as integral a part of Jeff's murder as the weapon itself. "Bringing the bed into the courtroom should not be that big a deal. That was the evidence. That was the way she committed the crime."

But some battered women's advocates who had warily watched the Wright trial, and found Susan's

claims of abuse believable, were outraged by both the
verdict and, especially, the way the murder had been
staged for the jury. In television interviews and angry
letters to the editor, they pointed out that it was un-
heard of for prosecutors trying a male defendant to
reenact something like a rape in court in order to convince the jury of the brutality involved.

For all of Siegler's assurances that she was within
her rights to reenact the crime, the fact remained that
it was sufficiently unusual that it was talked about on
a half-dozen national news shows in the wake of Susan's conviction.

In fact, the month after the Wright case wrapped
up, Siegler was back in another courtroom doing another demonstration with Paul Doyle—this time with
Siegler playing the part of the victim. The pair of
prosecutors acted out the details of a sexual assault
involving a church pastor and one of his female
parishioners that allegedly happened during a counseling session. Pastor Jim Tucker's attorney, Dick
DeGuerin, was a partner in Neal Davis' law firm and,
with the bedroom scene from Susan's trial fresh in
mind, he wasted no time in bringing the parallels to
the attention of Judge Michael Wilkinson. "Ms.
Siegler did this during the Wright case, which is probably going to be reversed because of it," DeGuerin
said, adding succinctly, "I object." Judge Wilkinson,
like Judge Wallace, allowed the demonstration to continue. Tucker eventually pled no contest to a lesser
charge, avoiding jail time in exchange for five years
deferred adjudication.

Attorney Ken McCoy would find himself being replaced in early October after another attorney accused

him of "dropping the ball" in the appeal that had been filed on Susan's behalf. It was an unusual eleventh-hour replacement, but Susan's family agreed and, after attorneys Brian Wice and Stanley Schneider also cleared their arrival with the court, they were allowed to refile Susan's appeal in November 2004.

"The brief that's been filed by her appointed lawyer was deficient in a number of aspects . . . [he] just basically, with all due respect, dropped the ball on the critical issue," Wice told KPRC Local 2 television news, adding "Kelly Siegler's production would have made any producer in Hollywood blush. Recreating the murder scene, bringing the bed into the courtroom, climbing on top of the homicide investigator, essentially [gave] the jury her theory about what happened."

In reality Hollywood rarely blushes, but it did sit up and take notice when Siegler made news headlines with her hard-hitting bit of courtroom theater. By the time Susan's appeal was being filed, producer Gina Matthews had already pitched to executives at ABC Television the idea of a *Law and Order*-type drama set in Houston and starring a character based on Kelly Siegler. The network loved the idea and promptly paid out a quarter of a million dollars to develop a one-hour pilot episode of the show to air during the 2005 fall season.

"The whole thing just screams, 'Television show!'" Matthews, who produced the *Urban Legend* horror movies, told the *Houston Chronicle*. Within days Matthews and Gary Glasberg, who had written the *Crossing Jordan* television series, were strolling through the courthouse in Houston and heading out to

Blessing, Texas, to meet Siegler's father and see where she had grown up, learning law as it was practiced in the feed shop.

Siegler wasn't the only attorney with experience in the media spotlight. Throughout the Wright trial Wice had been acting as a legal analyst and commentator for local and national television stations, and he'd made several comments about the demonstration with the bloody bed. Suddenly Wice found himself out of the stands as an observer and immersed right in the big game trying to get Susan a new trial.

"As soon as that demonstration was completed, the [prosecutors] sacrificed her right to a fair trial on the altar of high drama," Wice told the publication *Texas Lawyer* shortly after he filed the appeal.

In the same article Assistant District Attorney Paul Doyle, whom Siegler had sat on during the infamous reenactment, noted that Wice appeared to have changed his tune from what he was saying while he was a commentator. Wice responded that while he'd said it was a great show, he'd never said it was permissible.

In the new brief that Wice and Schneider filed with the 14th Court of Appeals in Houston, they argued that only Jeff and Susan had any firsthand knowledge of what had happened in their bedroom on the night of January 13, and anything the detectives and the state had to say about it was inherently speculation. Obviously, any inquest into such a murder would involve some level of speculation just by its very nature, but from a legal standpoint a courtroom demonstration can't stray even a little bit from witness testimony—and witnesses can only testify to what facts they can reasonably deduce from either firsthand knowledge or the evidence that they have collected.

The danger inherent in any demonstration is that, however well intentioned the whole thing might be, it runs the risk of filling in details that aren't actually in evidence. For instance, the jury might just assume that Jeff had been restrained that tightly because Doyle had been restrained tightly. The jury might not question whether Jeff had been screaming during the assault because Doyle hadn't been screaming during the demonstration, and on and on.

Despite their objections to the spectacle, if they were going to prevail in the appeals court—something that happens fewer than one in ten times when appeals are brought in non-death penalty cases in Houston— the lawyers would have to have a compelling legal argument.

In their new brief, Wice and Schneider argued that Siegler's reenactment had violated both the due process rules—a point that McCoy had raised in his original appeal brief—and the Texas Rules of Evidence, which spell out who can present what evidence to a jury. Specifically, they argued that Judge Wallace should not have overruled Neal Davis when he objected in court on the grounds that the demonstration violated Rule 602.

Rule 602 says that no one can testify as a witness unless evidence is introduced that is sufficient to show that he or she has personal knowledge of the matter. Wice and Schneider were arguing that, while the detectives could have testified to what they found out about the body and the bed, they had gone too far when Siegler hopped on it and effectively vouched for what she thought must have happened.

The attorneys' brief went on to argue that even if the 14th Court decided that Rule 602 hadn't been violated, then the whole thing still ran afoul of Rule 403, which allows even relevant evidence to be excluded "if its probative value is substantially outweighed by the danger of unfair prejudice, confusion of the issues, or misleading the jury . . ."

"Only by viewing the DVD of the staged in-court reenactment, a real-time production of the most violent part of the blockbuster *Basic Instinct* that was clearly the most defining moment of this trial, can this Court get any real sense of how and why its ability to impress jurors in some irrational but nevertheless indelible way is so far beyond any typical situation that it is impossible to see any way in which its misuse could be corrected," Wice and Schneider argued in their brief.

The attorneys cited a California Supreme Court opinion that warned of the dangers of using reenactments to present evidence. "Such a portrayal of an event is apt to cause a person to forget that 'it is merely what certain witnesses say was the thing that happened' and may 'impress the jury with the convincing impartiality of Nature herself,' " the California justices wrote.

Susan's appeal didn't rely strictly on the argument that the rules hadn't been followed properly and therefore she should be given a new trial. The appeal brief argued that not only did the demonstration have the *potential* to be unfair and misleading, but that it had *actually* been both of those things.

Susan's new attorneys noted that there was some testimony during the trial that Jeff had what appeared to be defensive wounds on his hands, but that would have been impossible if he had been tied as tightly to the bed as the state had demonstrated. In addition, Detective Reynolds had testified that he hadn't noted any bruises on Jeff's wrists or ankles indicating that he'd struggled to free himself from the ligatures. That could reinforce the defense theory that he'd been stabbed before Susan tied him down. These were the kinds of discrepancies that Wice and Schneider thought the jury would have picked up on if they had just been listening to testimony as opposed to watching a staged play, and these were facets of the evidence that couldn't be shown during the demonstration.

The bottom line of the appeal process, which was under way in the spring of 2005, was that either way it was a gamble for Susan. If she lost, she would not be out of prison until she was 40 years old. If she won, she would likely only win a new trial, and a new jury could still listen to all the same evidence and turn right back around and convict her again. And they would have the right to give Susan even more prison time than the first jury had. It was a risk Susan was willing to take.

30

Six weeks after the trial concluded, CBS's evening
news magazine show *48 Hours* took a look at the
Wright case in an hour-long episode entitled "Right
or Wrong?"

The most remarkable piece of news to emerge
from the show was Susan's sister Cindy Stewart's assertion that they both had grown up in a household
with a secret history of family violence.

"Love and pain are synonymous in our family,"
Stewart told CBS reporter Richard Schlesinger.

Cindy described incidents in which she said her
father kicked her in the back and the abdomen as she
lay on the floor because those were places on the
body where injuries wouldn't show in public. She alleged that both she and her mother were subjected to
that type of abuse while Susan watched, but said she
didn't specifically remember if it had also been directly inflicted on Susan.

In separate interviews both Kelly Siegler and the
Wrights indicated they'd always had an inkling that

there was some sort of secret about Susan's past which she never discussed.

In the *48 Hours* piece Stewart said that by coming forward with that information in an effort to help put Susan's actions in context, she was at the same time effectively severing all ties with her parents. Schlesinger said that in off-camera conversations, both of the Wyches denied their daughter's allegations that there had been domestic violence in their home when she was growing up.

"I understood why she stabbed him so many times," Stewart told Schlesinger. "She stabbed Jeff for all of the times that he punched her in the chest, and she stabbed him for all of the times that he raped her in the middle of the night. And she stabbed Jeff for my father."

In an exclusive jailhouse interview with Susan that aired during the same program, Schlesinger found that she had been shocked by the way the verdict came out.

"I just assumed that because what I was saying was the truth that everyone would believe it," Susan said.

She said she had watched the prosecution thinking all the time, " 'That's not true. That's not true. That's not what happened.' Because it's not. It wasn't anything like that. There was a struggle, there was no seduction, not any of what she made it out to be. That wasn't true, and it was horrible to hear."

Cindy Stewart also expressed amazement at the outcome and the fact that jurors had doubts about whether Susan was really a victim of domestic violence. "I had no idea how anyone could look in her eyes and listen to her and not believe her," Stewart said, adding at another point in the interview, "We would see her with black eyes, bruises all over her arms and legs, her back too sore to pick up her children."

When speaking to Schlesinger, Susan stood by the version of events she had given during the trial. "I was terrified because he was gonna kill me. I knew the second that I stopped, he was gonna get the knife back, and then I was gonna be the one that would be dead," Susan said.

"Do you regret killing Jeff?" Schlesinger asked.

"There are days that I miss him, but, like I said, that night he was going to live or I was," Susan answered.

"There are days you still miss him?" Schlesinger repeated.

Susan replied haltingly, "It's hard to just say, 'Okay, I don't love him anymore.' "

31

As unfair, as pointless, and as devastating as most murders undoubtedly are, it remains a peculiar fact of American life that murders are also one of the most common themes of our entertainment culture. Autopsies and crime-scene investigations used to be obscure rituals that weren't even mentioned in polite society, but now they are nightly fodder for some of the most popular entertainment programming in America. Millions of people watch the most intimate secrets and detailed methodologies of gruesome murder investigations for fun. It's been estimated that by the age of sixteen, the average American has watched at least 33,000 homicides portrayed on television alone.

What's even more strange than the sheer volume of slaughter that is viewed on the tube each night in the name of storytelling is what happens when real killings do occur and real trials are held. There is sort of an unspoken code that not only are defendants presumed to be innocent, but that the truly innocent would not have the faintest notion how to carry out complex criminal schemes—even though Hollywood and the networks have now spent several decades running what amounts to a twenty-four-hour, seven-day-a-week training course on that subject. Anyone planning a premeditated murder of a spouse and looking for the right circumstances to strike could be expected to take that kind of freely available information into mind.

It's a peculiar vestige of this country's Victorian past that women especially are judged against a kind of idealized formula of innocence that couldn't really exist in an age of television and media saturation. It's kind of the criminal justice equivalent of the good girl–versus–slut paradigm—If you didn't kill him, then you're the kind of girl who couldn't even hurt a fly; if you're the kind of girl who could hurt a fly, then you must have killed him.

In fact, for all the hand-wringing about whether violent television causes violence, it's pretty amazing there are as few murders out there as there are.

Against that backdrop it's worth stepping back for a moment and thinking about what else Susan Wright could have done if she had set out to kill her husband and get away with it.

The notion that Susan-the-Former-Topless-Dancer staged a naked seduction with neckties and then tied up and killed the helpless husband has a very Mata Hari–type feel to it, but if she needed to strike when he was helpless, she could have gotten him in his sleep with a lot less effort.

Killing him at home would make some sense in a premeditated murder plot, simply because it would have provided the most convenient opportunity. Stabbing him, however, would be about the worst choice to carry out a planned killing. Horrific, brutal, drawn-out, extremely messy, requiring physical strength and stamina, placing the attacker within arm's length of a victim who could be expected to fight back to save his life—all things which explain why so few premeditated murders are carried out with edged weapons. So few, in fact, that when murder victims are found with a frenzied number of stab wounds, it's almost automatically assumed that they were the victim of a rage-driven "overkill" by someone who knew them intimately and was extremely angry with them—not scared.

If Susan had suffocated, strangled, or poisoned Jeff that night, she wouldn't have had to clean and redecorate the crime scene and replace the bed. Just removing the lifeless body from the house would have been sufficient.

She may not be a criminal mastermind, but she did have all the tools at her disposal to have pulled off a much better cover-up than she did. She had Jeff's pickup truck and she did have a dolly. With something other than a massive stabbing she would've had all evening to dress the body in street clothes, wrap it up in a sheet, put it in the pickup, and dump it in some clever predetermined location at 4 A.M.

Susan knew full well Jeff was using cocaine, and if she was plotting all this in advance it would have occurred to her that if Jeff died on a night when he was high, this information would come out at an autopsy. She could have dropped his body off in a red-light district or an area where drug activity was known to take place, and then who could say why he met his end?

If the body had been dropped off somewhere in the vast city that is Houston, then once it was discovered Susan could have made up any story she liked—that she'd last seen Jeff storming out the door in a rage or heading out to buy cocaine, despite her objections. Police could have been as deeply skeptical of her as they liked, but, if everything went as planned, she would have had a good chance of avoiding prosecution—and there would be no real reason she couldn't stand there with two young children and demand prompt payment of her husband's $200,000 life insurance policy.

As it was, she actually did the one thing that would have made it *impossible* for her to collect on Jeff's insurance—she hid his body. How was Susan going to file a claim with Jeff buried out of sight under her patio?

Within minutes of killing him, she told relatives he'd left home in a rage—not something for which an insurance company was going to write her a check. Was she going to dig him up at some point when the coast was clear, drag his corpse down to the claim adjuster's office, and try to cash in his chips?

If Jeff had gone mysteriously missing, and stayed missing, Susan would have had to wait seven years to file a presumed death claim with the courts in order to get a delayed death certificate issued. Only then could she have started the ball rolling to try to collect on his insurance.

On the other hand, if Jeff had died in some sort of suspicious accident, or even if his murdered body had been found in some bayou clear across Houston, things would have been different. All kinds of people might have had dark suspicions. Susan might have faced some tough questions. But if nothing could've been proven, she would in all likelihood have gotten the check.

Instead Susan put a knife into Jeff almost 200 times in her own bedroom, in the process creating an unholy mess that would've required a complete remodeling job to clean up—let alone cover up. If it was a premeditated killing for financial gain, then it was one of the worst-thought-out ones in the history of insurance fraud.

Susan, the cool, calculating killer, who supposedly was willing to risk life in prison for a return in the low six figures, was actually undone by a chow-mix dog who kept digging up Jeff's body faster than she could keep reburying it. The prosecution had argued that Susan was prepared to kill the father of her two children, a man she had been married to for four years, all because she wanted cash. Yet, even after all that, when one dumb dog threatened to unravel her scheme and thereby cost her all the money, a life on easy street, and custody of her children, *and* potentially send her to the slammer for the rest of her life—what was her fiendish response? She caved in, confessed to both the killing and being in over her head, and had her mother hire a lawyer.

Would a woman who was prepared to kill off the father of her children for cash really hesitate to get rid of the dog too, because that wouldn't be "a Christian thing" to do?

The real question facing the jury was, what would a reasonable person do under those circumstances? Would a traumatized woman who had really just been threatened with violence, raped, and suddenly threatened with death fight back, kill, and then pause to tie up her attacker? What *is* the reasonable thing to do under those circumstances?

If Susan had been bolted down tight in the first place, would she have stuck with Jeff through four years of escalating violence and a spiraling dependency on drugs that were making him crazed? Did the fact that other women in the same circumstances would have picked up the kids and walked out the door make Susan more or less likely to be guilty?

The absolute core of the Susan Wright case was that period of probably less than three hours between the time that Jeffrey Wright pulled his pickup truck into the driveway on the evening of January 13 and the moment that Susan finally put down the bloody knife and stepped away from his body. Everything in Jeff and Susan's life before those hours and everything Susan did in the week that followed were only of interest because of what each side thought could be learned that would inform the jury's decision about the actual circumstances of the killing.

The real puzzle in so many mysteries is that, while having a specific piece of evidence can often prove that something did happen, lack of a specific piece of evidence doesn't necessarily prove that something *didn't* happen. Jeff's mutilated body was proof positive that he had been stabbed to death. The cocaine in his bloodstream was proof that he had been snorting the drug the night he died. Susan's story that he had beaten Bradley, raped her, and come at her with a knife was an open question. Maybe those things had happened exactly the way Susan said they did. Maybe it was sort of like that, but not quite. Maybe Jeff walked through the door that evening in a good mood and nothing remotely untoward took place until Susan tied him up and whipped out a knife. That brief early evening period in the Wright household was the one interaction between husband and wife that really mattered to the jury—and that was the one point for which there was not one shred of hard evidence pointing in either direction.

Although the discussion about them only took a brief moment during the trial, it's hard to overstate what a critical difference the fingernail scrapings could have made to the outcome of the Wright case.

When you think about it, there was some evidence to back up almost every single claim Susan made about the night Jeff died. She said he'd hit Bradley. Bradley corroborated that. Prosecutors argued that Bradley was either coached to lie or else it wasn't really abuse, just a father "play-boxing" with his young son. Nonetheless, the evidence on its face is that Bradley sat in a police station and told investigators that his dad had hit him.

Susan said Jeff was hyped-up on cocaine that night, and the toxicology tests came back showing that Jeff had indeed had coke in his bloodstream. Prosecutors argued that that didn't mean that Jeff had raped Susan and threatened her, but actual witnesses said that Jeff would become prone to violent outbursts when he was taking drugs. The point is, Susan

had claimed Jeff was on cocaine and it turned out to
be true.

The third thing Susan claimed about that evening,
and certainly the most important from a legal standpoint, was that she and Jeff had struggled violently
for possession of the knife and that the scratches on
her hands and bruises on her body were acquired during that fight for her life. Susan did show up at a police station less than forty-eight hours later and she
did have visible injuries on her hands and arms,
which were documented. Prosecutors argued that she
could just as easily have gotten the injuries from
nicking herself with the knife as she hammered it into
Jeff, since she'd been in the midst of a frenzy sufficient to break off the end of the blade. That's possible, but nonetheless Susan said that she'd acquired
minor injuries during the course of a struggle with
Jeff, and police have photographs showing that she
did have some.

The kicker is that the police actually had the final
clue in the set that could have provided an exculpa-
tory tipping point for Susan Wright. They had Jeff's
corpse, and they had Jeff's hands—the one that was
still attached and the one the dog had pried loose.
Forensic pathologists in the performance of their
grisly duties had carefully removed the "scrapings"
from underneath Jeff's fingernails, and if they had
just stored them properly and been able to test them,
they would have been able to clearly answer yes or no
to a simple question: Did any of Susan's skin end up
underneath Jeff's nails?

If it hadn't, then it would have been unlikely that
her injuries had been sustained in the manner she

claimed. Therefore the other things she said would be cast under similar doubt. But if the tests had come back positive, then however and whenever Jeff got the neckties around his wrists, it would have had to have been after he and Susan had struggled.

The one thing Kelly Siegler had convincingly demonstrated to all of Houston was that if Jeff had been tied down the way detectives thought, then there was no possible way that he could have gotten his hands anywhere near Susan during the attack, and he certainly couldn't have raked his fingernails into her enough to remove surface skin.

The whole case actually boiled down to one question and it wasn't the question of whether or not Jeff had been tied up. It was the question of whether or not he'd had the neckties attached to his wrists *before* he'd been stabbed the very first time.

Letting the fingernail scrapings get moldy was a colossal blunder. If Susan were truly innocent, if she had acted in self-defense that night, then those tiny samples were the only item in the entire Berry Tree Drive crime scene that had the potential to set her free. In fact, if the test results had come back showing significant amounts of Susan's skin cells underneath Jeff's nails, then even the grand jury probe that ended up taking her to court might well have gone differently. The grand jury had been looking for a fair and impartial way to back up her side of the story. They had even subpoenaed Bradley's medical records. Anything they could have found in the past indicating abuse would have helped them weigh Susan's tale in a more favorable light. But the one thing the state could have done to bolster Susan's case—the one thing that potentially had the power to prove her side of the story—was the one thing they screwed up.

But just because one little piece of evidence had gone moldy, the prosecution was not about to forfeit a trial they thought they could prove in any one of a dozen other circumstantial ways—and the defense couldn't afford to bet Susan's future on a clue that could have been.

The whole affair of the fingernail scrapings was reminiscent of the Louise Woodward trial in Boston in 1997. In that case a 19-year-old British au pair was accused of shaking an eight-month-old baby boy named Matthew Eappen to the point that he sustained a fatal skull fracture. Although the trial is remembered for its all-star legal team and numerous dramatic twists and turns that riveted two nations for months, what got overlooked in the shuffle of competing theories and scientific expert testimony was that if the coroner's office hadn't lost the very fragment of the boy's skull that contained the fracture, there could have been a clear, final answer as to whether or not the injury had occurred on the day that Woodward was caring for the boy. The jury initially convicted Woodward of second-degree murder, but in short order, in large part because of the lingering doubts, the judge in the case reduced her conviction to involuntary manslaughter and adjusted her sentence down from life to time served.

The trial of Susan Wright had revolved entirely around two opposing versions of what had transpired on the evening of January 13, 2003—but there were other possibilities.

Siegler's version was that Susan had coldly and calmly carried out a devious premeditated scheme to murder Jeff for financial gain. Susan's version was that she suddenly found herself in a life-and-death struggle and successfully defended herself.

But what if there had been no struggle for the knife and also no advance plot to kill Jeff? What if Jeff had been a miserable jerk that evening and was high on coke? So what? Susan had stayed with him through four years and had two children with him. There was no particular reason to believe her story that this night of all nights was the straw that broke the camel's back and forced her to issue a rage-inducing ultimatum. Perhaps the couple just decided to overlook their differences once again and have sex, replete with a little bondage game involving neckties. It might not be everybody's idea of a good time, but it was at least as plausible as either a "complete psychic break with reality" or an "unfathomably calculating murder plot."

What if, either shortly before or shortly after tying up Jeff with the neckties, it was Susan who had suddenly become enraged by something Jeff had said or done? Clearly she did the stabbing, but the motives presented to the jury by the two sides left the killing characterized as either a cool murder for cold cash— hardly the kind of thing that requires an overkill stabbing—or a violent overreaction to being terrorized and attacked, which in turn does not require an elaborate five-day cover-up.

It was possible that no struggle had taken place that would give rise to justified self-defense, but that in the midst of a miserable situation and confronted by a belligerent coked-out jerk, Susan had become enraged and moments later set out to kill Jeff. Since that scenario would also meet the criteria for a murder, albeit perhaps one rising from sudden passion, it's not like Susan wouldn't have been in real legal trouble either way.

The other possibilities start to matter when you consider what the jury's decision-making process would have likely been if they'd been asked from the beginning to choose between self-defense and sudden passion, with its 2- to 20-year sentencing structure, as opposed to either self-defense or a devious "black widow" murder plot.

Instead of asking the jury to consider between white and a shade of gray, prosecutors had effectively asked the jury to consider between white and black. By arguing that Susan was a plotter and a planner, the jury was put in a position where, if they didn't quite believe an element of Susan's testimony, or the rationale behind one of her actions, then the needle had to swing clear over to the other side of the meter.

As it was, the jury was asked to decide whether they were dealing with Snow White or the Wicked Witch, not whether they were looking at the actions of a suburban housewife who'd had her buttons pushed once too often.

The sheer number of times Susan stabbed Jeff had the effect of reversing the burden of proof in the case. Susan had to prove that she wasn't the kind of person who would enjoy doing in her husband in an orgy of bloodlust, because that's exactly the first thing that 200-plus stab wounds bring to mind. However, Susan's actions in killing Jeff, in burying him on the patio, and doing a completely inept job of explaining his disappearance, all pointed to someone making it up as they went along, not to someone executing a carefully premeditated plan.

The prosecution was in no mood to cut Susan any slack on Jeff's killing. They took a look at the 193-plus stab wounds, a week spent telling fishy stories about how Jeff had taken off, and the clean-up efforts, and they concluded they were not looking at an act of self-defense.

The problem for Susan was that the only legally acceptable defense she could present would have been pure insanity or pure self-defense—and neither seemed to fit her actions after the killing so her defense appeared to end up weaving an intricate version of both. It could even be believed on individual points, but, when taken as a whole, it seemed to be an implausible concoction of events.

One or two weird things, maybe—but to believe Susan, the jury would've had to believe thing after thing after thing that didn't add up. Still, if the jury really felt Susan was the bad person in this mix, why would they have given her one of the lightest possible sentences? The jury seemed to have a great deal of sympathy for Jeff's family, breaking into tears themselves as they listened to the Wrights, but their lenient treatment of Susan didn't seem to square with how they would have been expected to rule if they truly believed the prosecution's version of events.

It was as if, after spending nine days listening to testimony and evidence, the jury sensed that neither the prosecution version nor the defense version was a completely accurate reflection of what really happened that night.

The main problem with the prosecution version is that it assumes real premeditation on Susan's part—an advance plan to lure and kill Jeff at his most vulnerable. But nothing Susan did, from supposedly choosing a multiple stabbing as the murder method, to immediately dumping the body in a wholly inadequate hiding place right smack in the middle of her own house, gives any credence to the existence of a coherent scheme, let alone a successful one.

The main problem with Susan's defense was that she simply couldn't credibly explain how neckties, bathrobe sashes, and red candle wax were on Jeff's body if there wasn't a sex game under way, when everything from the physical size difference between her and her husband and the pattern of the stab wounds seemed to clearly indicate that Jeff had to have been restrained when the stabbing took place.

The difficulty with both the prosecution and the defense versions is that they both assume that *something* preceded the stabbing that night. The prosecution assumed that a devious scheme to kill was already afoot. The defense assumed that a raging attack by Jeff came first.

What if neither version is completely accurate?

There is a third scenario that seems to better fit the evidence than either of those two versions of the evening's events.

What if Susan's actions in the hours and days that followed the killing were exactly the kind of flailing, made-up-on-the-spot, disorganized efforts that they appeared to be, because she had no idea prior to the evening of January 13 that she would need to conceal a murder?

If Jeff and Susan had gotten into bed that evening, with or without a prior argument, but with every intention of having sex, and Jeff had allowed himself to be tied up with his own neckties to the bed frame, that would explain how he had come to be so restrained. What if Jeff had said something to Susan before, during, or after sex while he was still bound to the bedpost, not in a million years thinking that it would enrage his wife to the point she was willing to kill? What if he had, in fact, caused Susan, who clearly had any number of reasons to be dissatisfied with him and their relationship, to snap right in the middle of what Jeff had thought, up to that point, had been a pretty good evening?

If Susan suddenly went off the deep end and four years of pent-up frustration suddenly came pouring out at the point of a knife—if in previous days and weeks and months Jeff had been punching her and belittling her and controlling her and cheating on her and giving her venereal diseases and roughing up Bradley and spending their money on drugs and wrecking their finances—if it all finally became too much and, as he lay there tied up on the bed, the smug bastard had lipped off and she'd just completely lost it . . . then what?

For all of the smooth, careful, "one . . . two . . . three . . . four . . ." counting that Kelly Siegler did with the knife in court as she demonstrated the stabbing, it is actually possible to wham down a knife 193 times in about two minutes flat—you just have to be mad enough to expend the energy it takes to do it.

In the moments after the killing, it would have occurred to Susan that she couldn't just leave Jeff on
their bed. A natural reaction would be to get rid of
the horrible dead thing in the middle of the room.
Where could she put it? The most obvious place would
be the hole Jeff had dug for the fountain. It wasn't a
great solution, but it was the only one that was really on
hand. Calling Jeff's parents right away would be a
lousy choice for someone who was executing a careful plan, but it would make sense for someone who
was traumatized by what had just happened and
wanted to tell, needed to tell, someone what a complete jerk she thought Jeff actually was. Susan's family already had an inkling of what she thought Jeff
was like, but Susan knew the Wrights didn't know she
felt that way, and in fact she had expended a tremendous amount of effort for four years making sure that
they didn't find out. Now, with Jeff not even really
cold, the dam had burst and it was time to take it out
on them too, because frankly she felt they were part
of the problem. They'd raised Jeff. Jeff had been using her to play to them that he was such a great guy
just as he'd been using her wherever else he thought a
presentable wife and family would bolster his social
standing.

Susan couldn't very well tell the Wrights that she'd
just stuck Jeff two hundred times with a hunting
knife, so she conjured up a story on the spot that he'd
left the family for good. It was such a spur-of-the-
moment tale that it couldn't account for the fact that
he would've had to have left after dark on a side street
in a remote corner of suburban Houston, not bothering to take so much as his truck, his keys, or his cell

phone with him. If the events of the evening had been premeditated, there would have been no real reason to call the Wrights at all. Why start the stopwatch ticking on Jeff's disappearance any sooner than necessary? Why not figure out a way to get his vehicle and maybe a suitcase of clothes and toiletries to somewhere that at least wasn't his own driveway? For that matter, why plan to kill him on a Monday night when he would be missed when he failed to show up at work only twelve hours later?

But if Susan hadn't planned to kill Jeff that night, then why the cover-up?

Her story was always that it wasn't a cover-up at all. It was all supposedly a fog of post-traumatic stress that ended up producing goofy results. The prosecution delighted in pointing out over and over how the things she did after the killing appeared to be rational efforts at obscuring the truth of what happened. Well, maybe they were, but to the prosecution, that truth was always assumed to be an advance plot to kill Jeff. What if Susan's actions were those of a frightened woman trying to conceal the fact that she had suddenly become enraged and stabbed her husband to death as he lay tied up in bed in the middle of a sex game? Her actions in the five days that followed seem to better match that sort of scenario than either one that the prosecution and defense advanced.

Susan didn't seem to be acting like somebody who had just been forced to kill in self-defense. The appropriate response in that event would have been to pick up the phone and call 911 just as soon as she'd won the battle. Yes, there would have been a police investigation and a long, ugly night of explaining this to family and friends, but it would have been the logical response. But Susan also didn't seem to be acting like somebody who had just successfully murdered her husband in an effort to collect his insurance money. There just was no way that her actions, even if they had never been discovered, fit into any rational scheme to "get away with it."

In hindsight, Susan seemed to be reacting exactly the way that somebody who suddenly found themselves in the position of having spontaneously killed an abusive husband would have reacted. As soon as the killing rage passed, Susan would have immediately known she was faced with a tremendous dilemma. It would have occurred to her way too late that you just can't kill somebody because they've messed up your life and hurt you in the past, and then, this very evening, said something that really insulted, upset, or angered you.

Everybody knows you can't simply call the police and tell them that you just killed somebody because they had it coming. You have to have a good reason—and the only reason you can legally kill somebody else in the United States is that you are in reasonable fear of imminent serious bodily harm to yourself or someone else in your immediate vicinity.

There may well have been places and times where, if Susan had struck out and killed Jeff, she would have met that criterion, but on the evening of January 13 she could have killed Jeff when he was tied spread-eagle to a bed frame and there was no way that it was going to be seen as self-defense.

From Susan's perspective she would still not have viewed herself as the bad guy in that scenario, but she would know that legally she was in a world of trouble. So what would she do? She would try to think of something. She would try to buy time. She would take it hour by hour. She'd start with burying the body. She'd try to remove the bed to the back yard. She'd go back in and try to scrub, then try to use bleach, then try to use paint, then try to cut out the carpet, then try to report Jeff as missing, then try to explain things some more to worried relatives and inquiring friends and baffled co-workers and then—not being the least bit prepared to handle this kind of stress, and running five days without enough sleep, faced with trying to have to pull things together and having it all fail miserably, and then finally having a dog drag her dead husband's hand out onto the patio—she would collapse under the spiraling pressure.

That scenario seems to better fit the evidence and the testimony and the history of the relationship than anything either side presented in court. Ironically, it also seems to better fit the jury's decision when it came to Susan's sentencing. If the jurors had really believed in their hearts that Susan Wright had worked for days planning the vicious stabbing of her husband in order to collect insurance money and then she did it and then she nearly got away with it for five whole days until a dog just happened to get the better of her evil designs, it doesn't seem likely they would have given her the lightest possible sentence. Certainly not in the Texas justice system. Certainly not in Harris "Hang 'em High" County.

Whether they saw them all clearly or not in the five hours they discussed the case, the jurors seemed to sense the inherent contradictions that wove themselves

through both the prosecution and defense versions of
the murder, and they ended up splitting the difference. Their seemingly schizophrenic decision to nail
Susan for the crime and then largely let her off the
hook on the sentencing meant that in the end they effectively convicted her of the kind of lesser charge
that perhaps should have been brought in the first
place.